I Spy Books for All Ages:
I SPY: A BOOK OF PICTURE RIDDLES
I SPY CHRISTMAS
I SPY EXTREME CHALLENGER!
I SPY FANTASY
I SPY FUN HOUSE
I SPY GOLD CHALLENGER!
I SPY MYSTERY
I SPY SCHOOL DAYS
I SPY SPOOKY NIGHT
I SPY SUPER CHALLENGER!
I SPY TREASURE HUNT
I SPY ULTIMATE CHALLENGER!
I SPY YEAR-ROUND CHALLENGER!

Books for New Readers:
SCHOLASTIC READER LVL 1: I SPY A BALLOON
SCHOLASTIC READER LVL 1: I SPY A BUTTERFLY
SCHOLASTIC READER LVL 1: I SPY A CANDY CANE
SCHOLASTIC READER LVL 1: I SPY A DINOSAUR'S EYE
SCHOLASTIC READER LVL 1: I SPY A PENGUIN
SCHOLASTIC READER LVL 1: I SPY A PUMPKIN
SCHOLASTIC READER LVL 1: I SPY A SCARY MONSTER
SCHOLASTIC READER LVL 1: I SPY A SCHOOL BUS
SCHOLASTIC READER LVL 1: I SPY FUNNY TEETH
SCHOLASTIC READER LVL 1: I SPY LIGHTNING IN THE SKY
SCHOLASTIC READER LVL 1: I SPY SANTA CLAUS

And for the Youngest Child:
I SPY LITTLE ANIMALS
I SPY LITTLE BOOK
I SPY LITTLE BUNNIES
I SPY LITTLE CHRISTMAS
I SPY LITTLE LEARNING BOX
I SPY LITTLE LETTERS
I SPY LITTLE NUMBERS
I SPY LITTLE WHEELS

Also Available:
I SPY CHALLENGER FOR GAME BOY ADVANCE
I SPY JUNIOR: PUPPET PLAYHOUSE CD-ROM
I SPY JUNIOR CD-ROM
I SPY SCHOOL DAYS CD-ROM
I SPY SPOOKY MANSION CD-ROM
I SPY TREASURE HUNT CD-ROM

I SPY

SCHOOL DAYS

A BOOK OF
PICTURE
RIDDLES

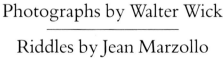
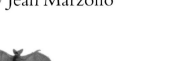

Photographs by Walter Wick

Riddles by Jean Marzollo

Cartwheel
·B·O·O·K·S·®

SCHOLASTIC INC.

New York   Toronto   London   Auckland   Sydney
Mexico City   New Delhi   Hong Kong   Buenos Aires

For my nieces, Heather, Jessica, and Emily,
and my nephews, David, Peter, and Michael

W. W.

For Marjorie Holderman, Joanne Marien, and Gerrie Paige

J.M.

Book design by Carol Devine Carson

Text copyright © 1995 by Jean Marzollo.
Photographs copyright © 1995 by Walter Wick.
All rights reserved. Published by Scholastic Inc.

SCHOLASTIC, CARTWHEEL BOOKS, and associated logos
are trademarks and/or registered trademarks of Scholastic Inc.

Library of Congress Cataloging-in-Publication Data

Wick, Walter.
   I spy school days: a book of picture riddles / photographs by
Walter Wick; riddles by Jean Marzollo.
      p.   cm.
   "I spy books"
   ISBN 0-590-48135-5
   1. Picture puzzles – Juvenile literature.   [1. Picture puzzles.]
   I. Marzollo, Jean.   II. Title.
GV1507.P47W528   1995
793.3 – dc20   94-43629

Reinforced Library Edition
ISBN-13: 978-0-439-68428-6
ISBN-10: 0-439-68428-5

10 9 8 7 6 5 4   7 8 9 10 11/0

Printed in Malaysia   46
This edition, March 2005

TABLE OF CONTENTS

Picture riddles fill this book;
Turn the pages! Take a look!

Use your mind, use your eye;
Read the riddles — play I SPY!

I spy a magnet, a monkey, a mouse,
A squash, two flags, five 4's, a house;

A bird on a B, an exit sign,
A UFO, and a valentine.

I spy a rabbit, a rhyming snake,
An apple, a shark, and a birthday cake;

An unfinished word, a whale, two dimes,
Tic-tac-toe, and JUAN three times.

I spy an acorn, a cricket, a 3,
A shell in a nest, a shell from the sea;

Three feathers, two frogs, a ladybug, too,
Ten drops of water, and thread that is blue.

I spy a frog, a checkerboard 3,
A zigzag 4, and a zebra Z;

A rabbit, an arrow, a girl named DOT,
Six red blocks, and the missing knot.

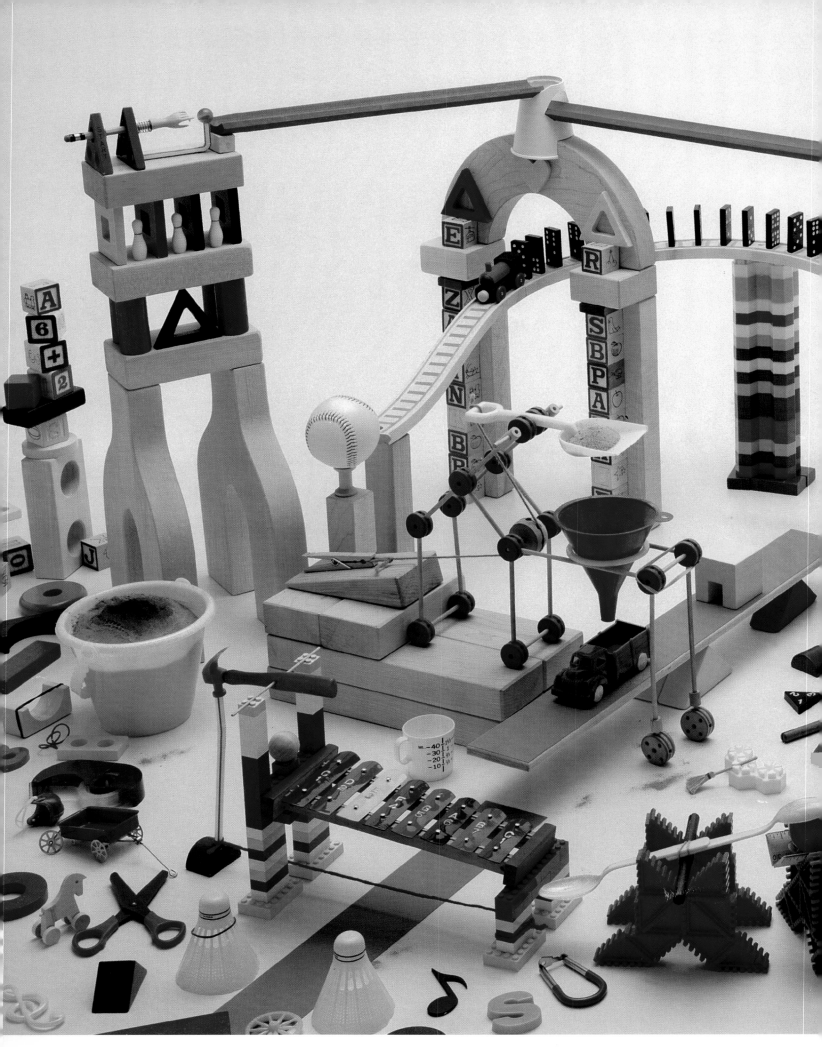

I spy a marble, a clothespin clamp,
FUN, two keys, and a ruler ramp;

Three helmets, a hand, a hammer, a heart,
A checker, a chair, and a chalkboard chart.

I spy a schoolhouse, three camels, a bell,
A lighthouse, a swan, and a basket that fell;

A paintbrush, a drum, an upside-down block,
A calendar card, and a grandfather clock.

I spy a mail truck, a valentine cart,
A blue eyeball I, and a five-button heart;

Six arrows, two horses, two airplanes, two clocks,
A key, and a card that is in the wrong box.

I spy a chimney, an anthill, a four,
A face with a smile, a star, and a score;

A feather, a twig, three footprints, a key,
A boat, two birds, a button, and BE.

23

I spy a walnut, two turtles, a pail,
Two eggs that are hatching, a clothespin, a snail;

Ten pinecones, an ant, a shovel, a plane,
A little red star, three frogs, and a chain.

I spy a kick ball, three ladders, and CLOCKS,
A small piece of chalk, four half-circle blocks;

A limo, a phone, and a rolling pin,
A flame, eight stars, and DEW DROP INN.

I spy three carrots, a magical hen,
Four keys, a candle, a cat, and a ten;

A teapot, a tin man, a rabbit asleep,
Anansi the Spider, and Little Bo Peep.

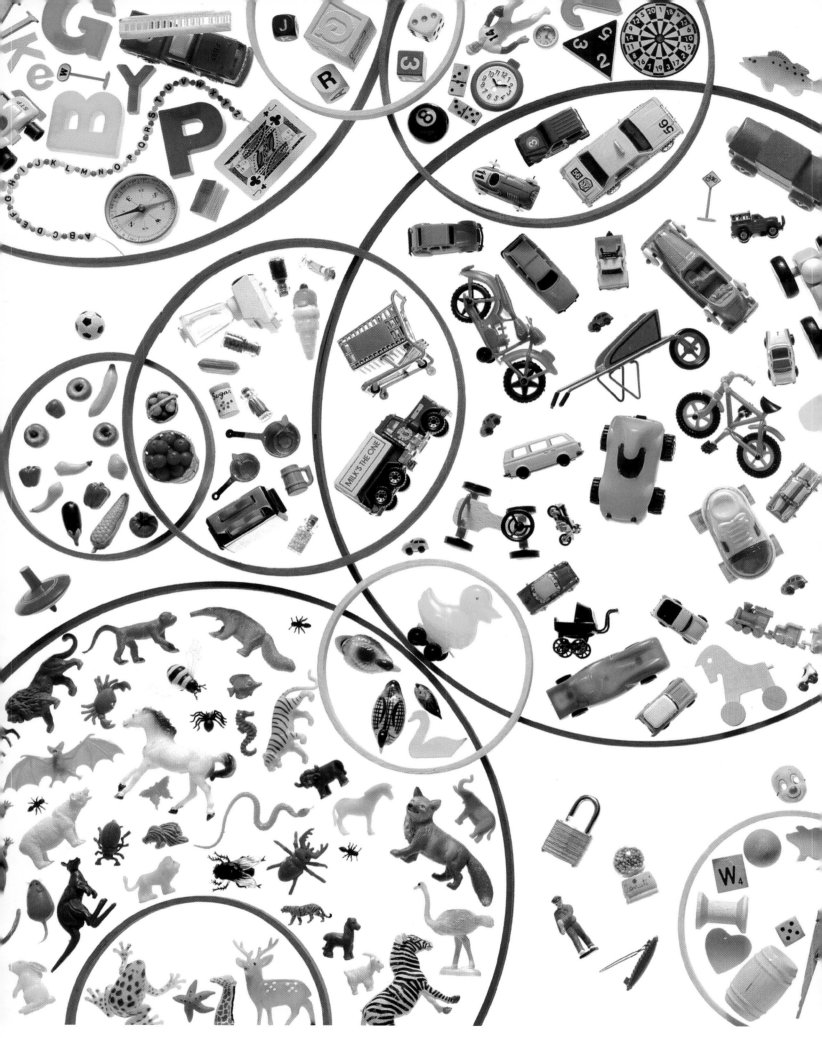

I spy a blender, a duck on a roll,
A pig, four bats, and a fishing pole;

Five barrettes and five yellow rings,
And places for all of the outside things.

I spy a spider, an ice skate, a rake,
Two bracelets that match, a trumpet, a cake;

A dime, the Big Dipper, three flowerpots,
A coat with four buttons, and ten paper dots.

EXTRA CREDIT RIDDLES

"Find Me" Riddle

I'm yellow; I buzz. If you look, you will see.

I'm in every picture. I'm a busy little _____.

Find the Pictures That Go with These Riddles:

I spy a ruler, a hanger, a wrench,

Eight traffic cones, and an empty bench.

I spy Rapunzel, a small piece of cheese,

A boy in a well, a bed, and some Z's.

I spy a starfish, a paper-clip chain,

A cow, seven hearts, and a yellow jet plane.

I spy a school bus, a camel, a lamp,

Two question marks, and a seven-cent stamp.

I spy a sea horse, a spotted cow,

Three butterflies, and the cat's MEOW.

I spy scissors and three striped cats,
Three pen points, and two yellow hats.

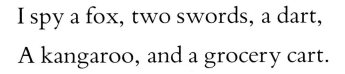

I spy a penny, a thumbtack that's red,
Two black ants, and a gray arrowhead.

I spy a fox, two swords, a dart,
A kangaroo, and a grocery cart.

I spy a feather and two equal signs,
A piece of pie, and three dotted lines.

I spy a truck, a shovel, a J,
Eight rubber bands, and some orange clay.

I spy a shovel, two rabbits, a yak,
A nickel, a knight, and a purple jack.

I spy a starfish, an uppercase I,
A pencil, a snake, and a dragonfly.

I spy a car and a speckled stone,
A chain, a seed, and a small pinecone.

Write Your Own Picture Riddles

There are many more hidden objects and many more possibilities for riddles in this book. Write some rhyming picture riddles yourself, and try them out with friends.

The Story of *I Spy School Days*

After visiting a number of schools where children and staff were successfully pursuing their own *I Spy* writing and art projects, Jean Marzollo and Walter Wick decided to create *I Spy School Days*. In order to celebrate the joy of intellectual discovery, the book has self-motivating and self-rewarding learning activities imbedded in the photographs. For example, when children look at the balloon-popper picture, "Levers, Ramps, and Pulleys," can they predict what will happen when the ball rolls down the chute? (By the way, after many trial runs, the balloon popper finally worked. Walter Wick made a video, recording the event.) When children study the picture called "Sorting and Classifying," they will discover that the circles contain different categories of things, but what will they deduce about the places where the circles overlap? How will they describe those sets?

Inspired by the eagerness of children to solve creative and intellectual problems, even at the youngest levels, Jean Marzollo and Walter Wick hope that *I Spy School Days* will inspire readers to be ever more curious, think logically, observe carefully, read and write interesting words, share ideas, work cooperatively, take risks, and make beautiful things.

Jean Marzollo and Walter Wick together conceived the ideas for the photographs in *I Spy School Days*. Then Walter Wick created all the sets for *I Spy School Days* in his studio, photographing them with an 8″ by 10″ view camera. As much as possible, he used ordinary classroom materials and familiar objects from the environment so that readers who desire to make similar projects can do so. As the sets were constructed, Jean Marzollo and Walter Wick conferred by phone and fax on objects to go in the sets, selecting things for their rhyming potential, as well as their aesthetic, playful, and educational qualities. The final riddles were written upon completion of the photographs.

Walter Wick, the inventor of many photographic games for *Games* magazine, is the photographer of *I Spy: A Book of Picture Riddles*, *I Spy Christmas*, *I Spy Fun House*, *I Spy Mystery*, and *I Spy Fantasy*. He is also a freelance photographer with credits including over 300 magazine and book covers, including *Newsweek*, *Discover*, *Psychology Today*, and Scholastic's *Let's Find Out* and *SuperScience*. Mr. Wick graduated from the Paier Art School in New Haven, Connecticut. This is his sixth book for Scholastic.

Jean Marzollo, a graduate of the Harvard Graduate School of Education, has written many children's books, including the *I Spy* books, *In 1492*, *In 1776*, *Ten Cats Have Hats*, *Sun Song*, *Pretend You're a Cat*, and *Close Your Eyes*. She is also the author of *My First Book of Biographies* and *Happy Birthday, Martin Luther King*. **Carol Devine Carson**, the book designer for the *I Spy* series, is an art director for a major publishing house in New York City. For nineteen years, Marzollo and Carson produced Scholastic's kindergarten magazine, *Let's Find Out*.

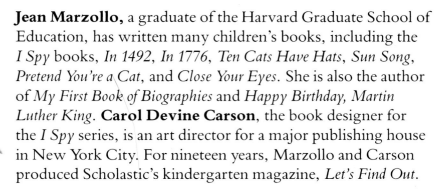

Acknowledgments

Again, we are grateful for the support and assistance of Grace Maccarone, Bernette Ford, Edie Weinberg, and many others at Scholastic. We also very much appreciate the help of Molly Friedrich at Aaron Priest Agency, Linda Cheverton-Wick, Elizabeth Woodson, Tina Chaden, Barbara Ardizone, Maria McGowan, Bruce Morozko, Frank and Ray Hills, Denis Gouey, Gator Laplante, and Lee Hitt. To Kevin Williams we extend a special thanks for his valuable and patient assistance throughout the entire *I Spy School Days* project.

Walter Wick and Jean Marzollo

DRAWING PEOPLE:
How to Portray the Clothed Figure

DRAWING
People

How to Portray
the Clothed Figure

Barbara Bradley

NORTH LIGHT BOOKS
CINCINNATI, OHIO
www.artistsnetwork.com

METRIC CONVERSION CHART

To convert	to	multiply by
Inches	Centimeters	2.54
Centimeters	Inches	0.4
Feet	Centimeters	30.5
Centimeters	Feet	0.03
Yards	Meters	0.9
Meters	Yards	1.1
Sq. Inches	Sq. Centimeters	6.45
Sq. Centimeters	Sq. Inches	0.16
Sq. Feet	Sq. Meters	0.09
Sq. Meters	Sq. Feet	10.8
Sq. Yards	Sq. Meters	0.8
Sq. Meters	Sq. Yards	1.2
Pounds	Kilograms	0.45
Kilograms	Pounds	2.2
Ounces	Grams	28.3
Grams	Ounces	0.035

Other fine North Light Books are available from your local bookstore, art supply store or direct from the publisher.

07   06   05   04   03   5   4   3   2   1

Library of Congress Cataloging in Publication Data
Bradley, Barbara (Barbara L.)
    Drawing people: how to portray the clothed figure / Barbara Bradley.— 1st ed.
        p. cm.
    Includes index.
    ISBN 1-58180-359-1 (hc. : alk. paper)
    1. Human figure in art. 2. Drapery in art. 3. Drawing—Technique. I. Title.

NC765.B72 2003
743.4—dc21   2003042043

Editors: Amanda Metcalf and Jennifer Kardux
Cover and interior designer: Wendy Dunning
Page designer: Kathy Gardner
Photographer: Elán Santiago
Production coordinator: Mark Griffin

DEDICATION

This book is dedicated to my two families.

To my first family: my husband Neil; our three children, Lauchlin, Glennis and Andy; their spouses; and our grandchildren, Diana and Lydia.

And to my second family, the many students I have taught and from whom I have learned.

ACKNOWLEDGMENTS

I wish to express my gratitude to the many people at the Academy of Art College who have been helpful and supportive and encouraged me throughout the development of this book. To Richard Stephens for first having urged this illustrator to teach; President Elisa Stephens, who carries on and enlarges upon the tradition established by her grandfather; my great friend Melissa Marshall; Howard Brodie, a great teacher and friend and an artist whom I have admired for so long; Director of Illustration Gordon Silveria; my ever-resourceful computer doctor James Volker; Jennifer Chang and Oliver Staeubli, whose technical labor and help saved me so much time; and the former students whose drawings you see in some of these pages. My special thanks go to fellow drawing instructors Diana Thewlis and Lisa Berrett, whose good sense and wise advice on choices of drawings, words and content were invaluable; and to photography instructor Elán Santiago, who enthusiastically and skillfully photographed hundreds of drawings for this book.

My thanks go to the many professional models who posed for me in various guises, especially Jesse Clark, Peggy Davis and Francis Kelly. I also appreciate the willingness of my three children and my elder grandchild who, in many modeling sessions throughout the years, have posed for me in gestures that were easy, hard and sometimes upside down, accepting all the while that modeling was what "kids in all families just did."

I also appreciate Willitts Designs, which allowed me to adapt drawings done for the company to include in this book; the staff of the Sutter's Fort State Historic Park and its docents, whom students and I have so enjoyed sketching; the members of the Terry Henry Jazz Trio and their guests, who combined sketching inspiration with great music; and the U.S. Air Force, which gave me wonderful experiences and the opportunity to draw USAF personnel during flights through its art program.

My further thanks go to North Light acquisitions editor Rachel Wolf and my editors, Amanda Metcalf and Jennifer Kardux, all of whom aided and guided me through the long process of bringing this book from imaginings to reality.

And last, but decidedly not least, thanks to my husband for providing his ample shoulder for me to lean on and for his forbearance during the many months when my mind was "on the book." It was he who said (and said at the right moment), "Don't put the book off. Start it now!" So I did and here it is.

TABLE OF CONTENTS

Library shelves are filled with wonderful books on drawing the nude figure, some of which have become classics but few about drawing clothed figures have been available. I have taught college courses on illustrative figure drawing for many years, but it was the response from professional artists during my drawing workshops that convinced me to create this book. My goal is to give artists greater control of the people they draw, wearing the clothing they want them to wear and telling the story they want to tell.

There are two things to consider as you draw figures. What are you trying to communicate; what opinion are you trying to convey through your drawing? Second, what principles and aides will you use to communicate that opinion?

Opinion—The What of a Drawing

Recall some drawings of people or figures that impressed you. Can you think of one factor common to all? An opinion is the common denominator of every drawing I greatly admire. I cannot recall a single one that did not reflect the opinion of the artist who drew it. Leonardo da Vinci uses opinion mildly in a study of folds for a seated figure. He uses the folds to create a beautiful design that reveals the figure in repose. Hans Holbein's opinion appears as he subtly suggests the personalities of his people in sensitive, beautifully designed portraits. Käthe Kollwitz's drawing of an anguished mother holding a dead child shows such passionate opinion that some viewers can barely look at it. Though the styles and subjects of these artists vary, the artists all showed opinion. You can almost hear them telling us what they saw and felt—how they related to the image—before drawing it and sharing it with us.

Opinion is the element of a good drawing for which one needs no art experience or education. Opinion comes from within us. Even young children have strong opinions about their subjects and drawings. What we see as scribbles, a child describes as an action hero zooming through space or the most beautiful of princesses. As adults, we should retain the enthusiasm children show us. Before every drawing, form an opinion. Your opinion about the person you are drawing, whether it is about the character, type, attitude, gesture or whatever else strikes you, is the goal of your drawing.

Principles and Aides—The How of a Drawing

The things we learn about drawing, whether from instructors, books, studying on our own, experimentation or emulation, all provide the know-how to communicate your opinions about the drawing. The drawing aides and devices emphasized in this book will help you do that. Understanding and practicing them will give you the control to portray your figures with authority.

Is There a Right Way to Draw the Figure?

No! There is no right way to draw the figure. To many students, different approaches to drawing seem to conflict. Instead, think of each approach as a different lesson with a different emphasis. All approaches are useful and all can be part of our never-ending study of drawing. After assimilating things you've learned, your brain, unbeknownst to you, puts everything together, developing the style that suits you best. Then, your own style can truly emerge, a unique combination of your own aesthetics, education and experience.

Only you know the purpose for which you want to draw people. Use this book and my suggestions as they are appropriate to your skill level, for your stage of development or for whatever subject you are most eager to explore.

1

TYPES OF FIGURE DRAWING

"WHEN YOU DRAW, DO YOU STAND UP OR SIT DOWN?"

Many guest artists visiting my classes have groaned inwardly when asked such a seemingly unimportant question. But when someone is learning and studying, anything that creates confusion, whether physical or mental, is important. Mental skills—the most important ones—develop from the accumulation of knowledge gained by observation and instruction. Physical skills are the technical ability to make your hands do what your mind tells them to. Artists must acquire both skills.

Let's start with the physical skills, drawing figures under different circumstances and for different purposes. Part one is about making everything that is physical—our media, our setups, our bodies and our hands—work for us. Controlling these factors will help you apply your accumulated mental skills to figure drawing in any circumstance, whether it's drawing from a model, sketching or drawing in your studio. Controlling the physical aspects of drawing will allow each type of drawing to flourish in its own way.

1

Drawing from a Model

Arrange an Effective Setup
This student has arranged her setup for a successful drawing session. She stands far enough from her drawing board to see all of her paper. She has placed her easel so she can see the model's entire figure. The flexibility of her hand as she holds her medium allows her to make strokes in any direction.

Artists use the marks they put on paper to express what is in their minds. The physical translation from head to hand is important in achieving that goal. Physical ease and flexibility allow artists' opinions to move from their minds and hearts directly through their arms, fingertips and drawing media to their paper. The greater the ease with which you can move your arm, wrist and hand, the less limited you are in your ability to express your opinion, what you want to say, about your subject. To clearly express their artistic messages, dancers and musicians must develop and control their physical skills. So, too, must an artist's hands and arms be ready to draw what his or her mind sees without being limited by a lack of physical skills.

If you can draw in large motions, the range of motion and ease of movement you acquire will carry over to smaller drawing motions. So this chapter deals with drawing models on large paper, including approaches to drawing, procedures, setups and drawing media that will help develop both physical freedom and control.

USING YOUR MEDIUM

Something as simple as the way you hold your drawing medium can make all the difference. Holding it correctly can increase your range of motion and the variety of strokes you are able to make. This, in turn, increases your ability to express what you want about a subject.

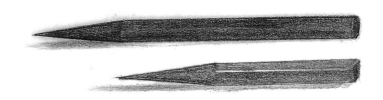

Soft Media Develop Flexibility

An artist who has wrist flexibility can use spit and a burnt match with some success. However, using short, soft media helps develop flexibility. Using a short medium will keep your hand close to the paper so you can feel a subject as you would a sculpture. With a soft medium the artist can make marks easily without bearing down. Sharpened media allow you to apply both line and tone easily.

Use a Sharp, Soft Medium

I recommend a soft stick medium, such as X-soft compressed charcoal or a pastel stick in a dark brown color. Conté Bîstre is a good choice. To sharpen it, make a long point on your medium with a craft knife, then smooth its sides on a sand pad so you have the choice of making a line using the tip of the medium or applying tone using the side.

Hold Your Medium Overhand

Let this be an order! Hold your medium overhand so you can apply strokes in any direction. With your palm upward, place the drawing medium perpendicular, not parallel, to the line of your fingers. As you draw, make sure it continues to lie across your fingers. If your medium is parallel to your fingers, it will get "stuck" and you won't be able to stroke in as many directions or change from line to tone.

Give Yourself Choices

Holding a sharpened medium overhand allows the flexibility to make strokes in any direction and switch between line and tone, even in a two-minute thumbnail like this.

FLEXIBILITY OF MOTION

Flexibility of your hand, wrist and arm enables you to place line or tone in any direction. The direction of your strokes should relate to the opinion you want to express and to the forms of the figure. Leonardo da Vinci chose to apply strokes in only one direction in many of his magnificent studies. However, you should use techniques like that only by choice, not because it is the only direction in which you can apply strokes.

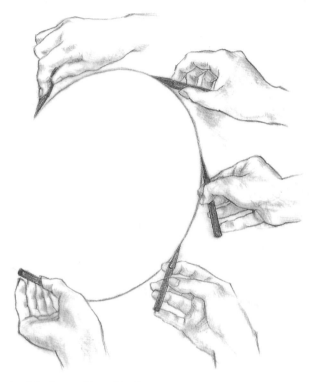

Use Your Entire Arm
Imagine the head of a pet poking through a hole in your paper. As you draw, feel the head as a sculptor would feel it. Move your fingertips across the paper from the far side, around the head and under the chin, paying attention to the movement of your arm. When your fingers are on the far side, your elbow is high. Under the chin, your elbow is tucked next to your body with your palm facing upward.

Apply the Motion to Your Medium
Draw an oval or circle, feeling the form as you did around the pet's head. Rotate your hand, wrist and arm as you draw.

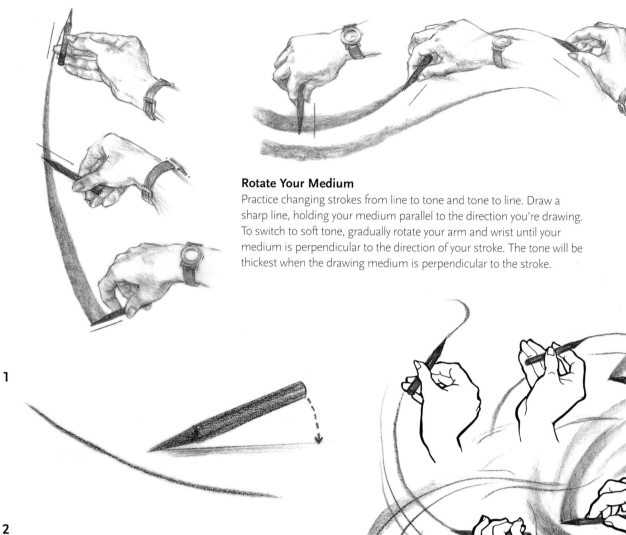

Rotate Your Medium

Practice changing strokes from line to tone and tone to line. Draw a sharp line, holding your medium parallel to the direction you're drawing. To switch to soft tone, gradually rotate your arm and wrist until your medium is perpendicular to the direction of your stroke. The tone will be thickest when the drawing medium is perpendicular to the stroke.

1

2

Adjust the Angle of Your Medium

Varying the angle of your medium to the paper is another way to vary the width of your stroke. A greater angle between the medium and the paper (drawing 1) produces a sharp line. A smaller angle (drawing 2) with more of the medium touching the paper produces a soft tone.

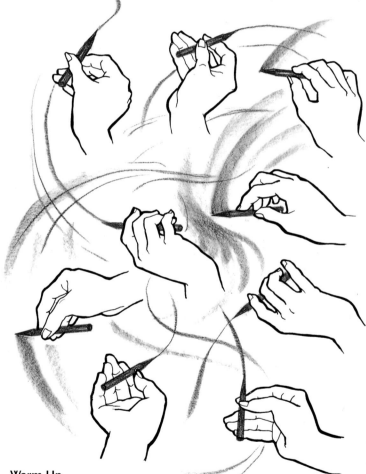

Warm Up

Warm up before every drawing session. Make strokes in every direction. Draw lines, tone and curves. Move your hand as though you were moving around a form. Have fun. Get flexible. After you have drawn for a while, examine your medium. If one side of the point is flat, you aren't rotating. If the sides are worn down evenly, you have been rotating your wrist exactly right!

POSITION YOURSELF COMFORTABLY

Here are some hints for drawing when standing at an easel or sitting on a drawing bench, both common positions for drawing a model:

- Make sure you can see the person you're drawing as easily as you can see your drawing. Place your drawing bench or easel at an angle so you can see your subject at the side of your drawing board.
- Use a drawing board to provide a firm drawing surface.
- Avoid tense shoulders by relaxing your hand while you're drawing and resting it downward while observing.

Standing at an Easel

Stand far enough from your paper so you can see your entire drawing. Adjust the easel's height so your eye level is about two-thirds of the way up the drawing. Try placing one foot closer than the other so you can easily rock back and forth to assess what you have drawn. Make sure you don't have to peek around the easel to see the model. The easel doesn't have to see the model. You do.

Sitting on a Bench

Position yourself far enough away from the paper to see the entire paper with ease. Sit upright so your arm is ready to move. Angle your pad behind the ridge on your bench so your eyes are perpendicular to the paper and you aren't viewing your paper in perspective.

Lifters

A lifter provides a higher ridge on which to place a drawing board, giving tall people more control when drawing on the lower part of their paper. You can build lifters easily.

Keep Your Board Off Your Legs

Place your bench at an angle to the model so you won't have to move your board to see. When drawing large, placing your board across your lap limits freedom of movement in your hand and forces you to view your drawing in perspective.

DRAWING DIRECTLY

When you draw an image directly on the paper without an under-drawing or visible guide, you are drawing directly. Drawing directly encourages you to look, to observe and to think. The only guides you should use to draw directly are in your head. They are the essential things you observed and intend to convey. These things form a mental map of where you want to go.

Drawing directly does not mean that you have to draw with one continuous line. It simply means that once you've gathered the information you need to draw something, you draw it. To draw with immediacy and freshness, develop drawing authority or draw a subject in twenty minutes or less, draw directly!

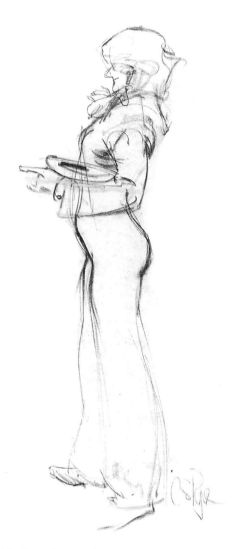

Try Drawing in Line

You can use line, tone, a combination of both or even mixed media to draw directly. Drawing in line is a wonderful discipline for learning because it teaches you to look and think. Student Chuck Pyle captured the sassy confidence of this mime with this two-minute direct line drawing. Though he barely indicated her face and hands, viewers notice her grin and the amusing way she holds her hat.

Acquiring Line Sensitivity

Lines in a line drawing can vary in weight, thickness and degree of sharpness. This varia-tion of line quality is called line sensitivity. It's the one quality of figure drawing that you can't acquire by thinking about it. Like love, it comes when you're not looking for it, when your acquired knowledge combines with a free and flexible hand to express your opinion. That is when line sensitivity comes naturally. Student Bill Sanchez did not use any guide lines and did not erase any lines in this twenty-minute drawing of a Scotsman. The wonderful sensi-tivity of his lines resulted naturally from his flexible hand's response to his careful observa-tion and the opinion he wanted to convey.

TELLING A STORY

I f you imagine your clothed model in a certain situation, time and place, you can make up a little story for yourself. The story you decide to tell and the things you want the viewer to notice will give you ideas for how to draw the figure. You can focus a viewer's attention with tone, detail and dark accents and even by leaving things out.

Use Tone to Convey Mood
Decide where tone will be most effective for your story. In this twenty-minute drawing of a blues singer, student Val Mina used tone to emphasize the theatrical lighting, but only on her face, accenting it with dark eyes and lipstick. He also accented her hands with the dark microphone. A few simple lines and a little tone on her torso complete the story.

Crop the Figure
One way to tell a story is to crop the figure to its essential storytelling elements. Student Kazuhiko Sano simplified this woman's clothing, directing the viewer's eye to the sensitive details of her apprehensive expression and nervous hands.

HINTS

Here are some hints that will help you improve:

- To practice full figures, draw the entire figure in poses of less than ten minutes. You don't need to be close to the model for these sketches.
- For twenty-minute poses, consider drawing a cropped section of a pose close up to improve your observation skills and to practice using storytelling details.
- Whether you like a drawing as a whole, consider it a success if you learned or observed something new.
- Make people at home your models. They may not be able to hold action poses, but you can practice many aspects of figure drawing even as a friend or family member naps or relaxes in front of the television.
- Draw yourself while looking in the mirror. You even can tilt a full-length mirror at different angles to get different perspectives.
- Invest in a lightweight easel, or make your own drawing bench by placing two chairs so they face each other.

Don't Worry

If you've never held your medium overhand before and you feel a bit out of control, don't worry. Your control may regress a bit at first, but your potential is higher than before. If you're discouraged, look for occurrences where your strokes show authority and flexibility. Practice these even more and you'll get the hang of it.

Last of all, don't worry about charcoal smears on your paper from dragging your fingertips. Developing flexibility is more important than creating a clean, pristine drawing. With practice you'll be able to avoid smearing and your drawings will look just the way you want them to.

Experiment With Different Media

Once you get used to a short, soft medium like charcoal, you also will feel more confident and comfortable with other media. When you can switch easily between the sides and the point of a charcoal stick, you'll be able to do the same with a charcoal pencil. From there, move on to other media: ink and brush, pastels or small brushes and diluted oils. Also try different surfaces.

Student Han Liu conveyed the above singer's mood in short poses of about three minutes. After establishing her attitude with compressed charcoal, he enhanced her satin-clad form with white chalk. In the drawing at right, student Paul Mica combined different media and techniques. He used colored pastels and light and shadow on her face and compressed charcoal to fill in the solid shape of her sweater. He used charcoal to draw her legs, clad in tights, with line.

2

Drawing in a Sketchbook

Drawing People Together
You can't anticipate how long a pair or group of unposed people will stay in position, so you may want to concentrate on one figure or one part of a drawing. But, you can be optimistic by leaving room on your paper for an additional figure or figures in case they've remained fairly still. I wanted to sketch these pioneers at a living history reenactment to capture the period clothing, and before they moved, I was lucky to capture both of them and start on the environment. I added more to their surroundings after they had moved.

You can sketch on anything: a sketchbook, a sketchpad, a piece of paper. Sketchbook drawing really is a type of drawing. Sketchbooks are great tools for collecting and recording information, forming ideas and keeping a journal. They are places where you can fill the library of your mind.

Sketches by master draftsmen from the Renaissance to today show a tremendous range of subject, style and quality. Some are so beautiful that artists are awed by them. Don't let these intimidate you. When you see drawings that are less than masterful, feel encouraged. When you see awe-inspiring drawings, learn from them.

I didn't begin to draw in sketchbooks until late in my career. At first I sketched to pass time whenever I was waiting during day-to-day activities, but it became one of the most pleasurable parts of my art. If you haven't yet begun to sketch in a sketchbook, I urge you to start. Sketching will become another tool for your enjoyment and learning. You can sketch anything or anyone who interests you; this chapter, however, concentrates on recording real people in real situations.

What should you draw? When drawing people, whatever strikes you about them is worth drawing. You may want to catch an entire scene with masses of people, or you may prefer to depict just one or two figures with a few props to set the scene. If a spontaneous gesture catches your attention, try to capture its essence. If a face intrigues you, draw the head. Though your priorities will differ for each sketch, the only thing you absolutely should do is draw a subject you want to draw.

Begin With a Head

I usually begin by drawing the head, hoping I can finish the figure. If the subject moves before I can capture the whole figure, as this pioneer did, at least I've caught something interesting in my sketchbook.

Capture People in Interesting Places

Sutter's Fort State Historic Park in Sacramento, California, is a great place to sketch. On Pioneer Days, costumed docents reenact typical fort activities of 1846.

Go Easy on Yourself

You can only guess how much time you'll have to sketch a person before he or she moves, so don't be concerned with drawing an entire figure, finishing any one drawing or making a drawing perfect. What is important is the observations you make. Relax! Care about what you observe. The mountain man in drawing 1 stayed still long enough for me to draw his entire figure and capture his attitude and exciting garments. That's enough to make it a successful sketch. The mountain man in drawing 2 moved around a lot. I wanted to make sure I recorded the authentic cut and baggy-kneed hang of his buckskin pants, so I began the sketch at his midsection. I didn't sketch his entire figure, but I recorded the detail I wanted and learned from the sketch.

1

2

SKETCHING MATERIALS

Whether you sketch in a sketchbook or sketch pad or on loose paper depends on where you're drawing. Always carry a small sketchbook with you so you can capture everyday sites and scenes. When you head somewhere with the specific intent to draw, take a large pad and any equipment you think you might use. No matter what kind of paper you use, make sure it's acid-free.

Hardcover sketchbooks serve as lasting journals of your drawing life. However, they do have a few drawbacks. You always have to draw in the same size book, and drawing in a bound book is awkward if you have to stand. Lefties also have to draw on the left page or work around the binding.

I prefer sketch pads with spiral binding on the top. Unlike sketchbooks, sketch pads aren't necessarily meant to hold a chronicle of your drawings and sketches, so I can work in a few different ones at once, selecting the type and size of paper appropriate for a drawing. They're also lighter and easier to hold than sketchbooks.

When You Plan to Draw

When you go somewhere planning to draw, such as an athletic practice, a dance class, a senior center or the living history site where I drew this sketch, equip yourself with a pad that is large enough—11" × 14" (28cm × 36cm)—and any sketching equipment you may use.

When You Happen to See Something

Carry a small sketchbook as you go about your daily activities so you'll be ready to record whatever appeals to you. You may find time to draw when standing in line, on public transportation or in cafés. I drew this gentleman patiently waiting to register his car while I less-than-patiently stood nearby in a long line. When you use a small sketch pad, people seldom notice that you're drawing.

Media

You can sketch with whatever you have handy or feel like using at the moment; it's all valuable experience. However, some media are better suited to certain circumstances: You can use pens and pencils at almost anytime or anyplace, but pastels and paints require room for equipment and a place to sit.

Pen is a fine medium for sketching. The permanence of pen lines may be frustrating to beginners, but it motivates artists to observe more before drawing, making it a great learning tool. I like a Micron Pigma with an O1 point. It's handy and lightweight, uses waterproof archival ink, and has as flexible a point as I can get on a disposable pen. I never recommend using a ballpoint pen.

With experimentation, you'll find other media you like, and your choices will continue to become more creative.

Other Equipment

The following equipment, which I've learned to take along from experience, may make your sketching experience a bit more comfortable and successful:

- folding stool
- light balsa or foamcore drawing board for support
- removable tape or clips for securing pages on windy days
- trash bag and rock for windproofing
- sunglasses, wide-brimmed hat, sun umbrella, sunscreen and drinking water
- water, towel and tissues for paint
- pencil sharpener and sandpaper
- an equipment bag to carry it all

Mixing Media
I used a brown pen to sketch this settler at a living history site. Next, I applied loose washes of watercolor, using local colors and value, over the sketch, modelling the face and depicting folds in her clothing. I also added a few pen lines for accents. The contrast of crisp line to fresh watercolor is satisfying and the technique is quick. Don't be afraid to try new media or combine unlikely ones.

DETERMINE YOUR PRIORITIES

Decide whether the purpose of a sketch is to observe and depict interesting detail, to capture the look of a person or gesture or to communicate the feel of the scene.

I drew these sketches of the Terry Henry Jazz Trio during their music sessions. When a musician was playing a short solo and moving around a lot, I concentrated on catching the action and spontaneity of the music. When my priority was to catch a more detailed likeness, I drew the musician as he played backup and thus stood more still.

Concentrating on Composition
My priority in this sketch was to design a composition of the interplay between the drummer and bassist. The complex scene of figures and instruments presented a challenge. I had to pay attention to areas where drums, cymbals and musicians overlapped.

Capturing Light
In this sketch I wanted to catch the effect of overhead light on the flautist's interesting face. I managed to catch his likeness and communicate the lighting to my satisfaction.

Capturing a Feeling
My priority for these quick sketches was to catch the musicians' intensity as they improvised solos. I had time only to indicate one of the trumpet player's hands, but I achieved the purpose of this sketch, letting his face and shoulders indicate his intensity.

Sketching Figures in Motion

The comment I hear most frequently about sketching figures in action is "They move too fast." You can eliminate such frustration by training your eye to take in increasingly more at one time. The more you can observe and appreciate at a glance, the faster you can draw and the more you can capture. With practice you can observe, appreciate and analyze the whole of an action and its essential parts in seconds.

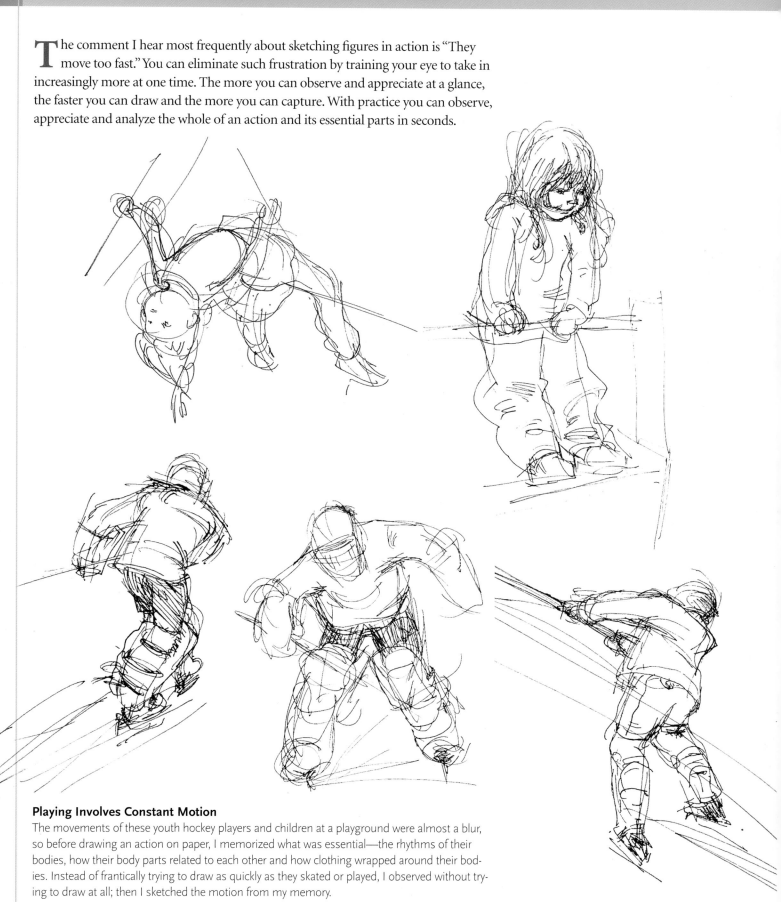

Playing Involves Constant Motion
The movements of these youth hockey players and children at a playground were almost a blur, so before drawing an action on paper, I memorized what was essential—the rhythms of their bodies, how their body parts related to each other and how clothing wrapped around their bodies. Instead of frantically trying to draw as quickly as they skated or played, I observed without trying to draw at all; then I sketched the motion from my memory.

Take the Time to Develop Drawings
This full-color watercolor is a cropped section of the finished art for a collector's plate, which I researched, composed, drew and painted in my studio.

CHAPTER

3

Drawing in Your Studio

In your studio, you could work on preliminary drawings for a specific project—from compositional thumbnails through a final draft—you could do experimental drawings, you could draw studies or a more advanced, finished drawing. For all types of drawing you can do in your studio, the common need is to be efficient and make the most of the time you've set aside to draw. In this chapter, I'll offer suggestions and show examples of my studio drawings at different stages.

Your Studio

Every artist's dream is to have a spacious, well-equipped studio with north light. But many artists, professionals and students alike, have produced beautiful work under circumstances far from ideal. Any place where you produce artwork becomes your studio, even if you don't have a door to hang a sign that says "studio."

To make the most of whatever space you have, try to get this equipment:

- drafting table with an adjustable board that can be raised, lowered and tilted to different angles. If the drafting table has a large surface, you can tape materials to it for reference.
- comfortable chair, preferably wheeled so you can glide around and turn quickly and easily
- overhead light and an additional adjustable light
- artists' tabouret. You can put your drawing materials on a side table, but this low cabinet is on casters and has drawers for materials, making it much more efficient.

My Setup
Place your tabouret on the same side as your drawing hand. (I'm left-handed.) I often see beginners awkwardly reaching across their bodies for their drawing media. If you can, use a nearby space for additional equipment, such as a bulletin board, shelving for books and reference and an electric pencil sharpener.

1

2

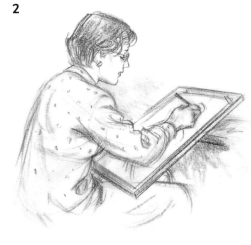

You Don't Need Much
This student makes do with a minimal setup: a chair, a portable drawing board and a table on which to balance her board and place supplies. She also could place a chair or small table at her right to hold additional materials.

Tilting the Drawing Board
When working large, as in drawing 1, tilt your board closer to vertical as if you are working on a drawing bench or easel. This assures that you won't be viewing your work in perspective and that you will have a free range of motion. When working small or on tight, finishing details, as in drawing 2, slant your drawing board closer to horizontal.

RESEARCH

Research can provide both information and inspiration. If you're drawing a period piece or a drawing set in a unique location, researching the place and time period of a scene is vital in composing your picture and providing authenticity. Clothing, props and the surrounding environment all provide shapes and masses and suggest situations and ideas unique to that time or place.

Researching to Get Ideas

In these sketches I was exploring ways an Amish girl might use a quilt. I noticed rag rugs in references about Amish homes, which gave me the idea to use the quilt on a rug. The idea of covering her doll in a child's chair led to the idea of playing peek-a-boo with a real baby. You might notice that the baby's body underneath the quilt is too long. Developing ideas was my priority at this stage, so exact proportions didn't matter.

Researching for Authenticity

My job was to draw a Navajo girl holding a hurt lamb. First I researched Navajo clothing. Then I did several thumbnails, exploring the different attitudes the girl might take. After I decided on this thumbnail, I photographed a child posing in that gesture and wearing clothing similar in shape to what I had found in my research. I had to use a baby goat, but she held the animal the same as a lamb, and researching the lamb enabled me to switch the animals in the final drawing.

Researching to Develop Composition

The intent of this sketch was to show an Amish family preparing its country stand for business. Research gave me a feel for the environment, the produce they might display and how they might display it. I sketched the food and containers to help commit them to memory so I could draw preliminary composition sketches like this one without looking at any reference. This early stage of the drawing required only a loose drawing. I was interested only in the picture's content and design here.

Using References From Research

The composition of this sketch is similar to the one above. Here I changed the smallest girl's gesture so she'd seem more involved in the family project. At this point, I hadn't used any models. I also concentrated more on the design and details of the produce. To help me work these elements out, I posted references on my drawing board so I could refer to them easily as I drew.

FOLLOWING A DRAWING PROCESS

When I was asked to create a water-color for a collector's plate, the company gave me the subject matter, an Amish girl sewing a small quilt at home, and the rest was up to me. Below are the steps I followed to develop the painting:

- researching
- developing idea and compositional thumbnail sketches
- drawing rough sketches
- posing and photographing models
- drawing the final pencil draft
- painting a paint rough, or draft, in the same medium as the final painting
- painting the final painting

Thumbnail Sketches

Thumbnails can hold the key to the ultimate success of a picture. Your priority in thumbnail sketches is to explore a narrative's composition—how the masses and directions of figures and elements relate to one another, to their locations and to the story you want to tell. Such sketches can start as blobs and squiggles that only you understand, or they can look more like these. Keep the compositional process free-flowing. I usually begin my thumbnails without a boundary, cropping to the proportion I need or want as I go. Thumbnail sketches, though usually small, can be any size as long as they avoid detail. After doing some research, I drew many composition sketches like these. I cropped the bottom right sketch to create another composition, which I chose for the final picture.

Value Sketches

Once I had chosen a composition, I did a few value sketches using that composition. This one indicates the lighting I wanted—a small amount of bright sunlight falling on the girl as she sits inside.

Final Pencil Drawing

If I'm drawing for a painting, I draw drafts using soft pencil on tracing paper the same size as the final painting. When I'm satisfied with the image, I draw a final pencil drawing on wrinkle-free vellum. I use a harder, well-sharpened pencil at this stage to define details. Then I transfer the drawing onto watercolor paper with a 5H pencil and begin painting. I lightly erase the transferred image and redraw it. This pencil image is my next to last version. The painting is the final word.

BASICS OF DRAWING

TO DRAW THE FIGURE WELL, IT'S IMPORTANT TO study principles of perspective and learn about anatomy. To control the appearance of the people you draw, you also must be aware of proportion. Learn about value so you can manipulate it to enhance form, communicate mood and direct a viewer's attention.

The chapters in Part 2 will introduce you to these aspects of drawing and the ways they can affect both the people you draw and the story you want to tell. The primary focus of this book is drawing people and their clothing, so these chapters will only introduce you to proportion, perspective, anatomy and value. I encourage you to study these subjects further on your own.

CHAPTER 4

Proportion and Perspective

Perspective Affects Visible Proportions
This little girl, drawn in Mexico, had proportions typical of her age. I viewed her from a close and high view, so perspective foreshortened her body, lower legs and feet, making them seem much shorter than if viewed at eye level.

Proportion is the comparative size of one portion of an object or person to another portion or to the whole. A figure is considered to be in proportion when its parts appear harmonious. Proportion is the aspect of figure drawing to which nonartists are most sensitive. They notice immediately if proportions seem wrong, making comments such as, "That figure looks funny," or more specifically, "Why is the head so big?" If a figure seems wrong to a viewer, it probably is.

Once you understand the proportions of figures as viewed from eye level, you'll be able to draw them from different views, or perspectives. Understanding the effects of perspective and ways to communicate these effects enables you to draw a person in the proportions and environment you want and from the perspective you want.

STANDARDS OF PROPORTION

Though standards of proportion have varied around the world from culture to culture and over time, artists always need a uniform standard of comparison for reference. The three most commonly accepted standards of proportion are normal, ideal and heroic.

To draw a figure in normal proportion, consider the average adult as seven and a half heads tall, with the hip joint about halfway up. Albrecht Dürer followed these proportions.

Leonardo da Vinci used ideal proportions, drawing figures eight heads tall. These proportions look realistic, but compared to them, a normal person's proportions seem dumpy.

Heroic proportions use figures that are nine heads tall. Michelangelo and John Singer Sargent managed to make heroic proportions appear realistic.

Ideal Proportions

I use ideal proportions to draw most of my figures. When I want to draw other body types, I compare them to this standard. This troubadour's height is eight times the height of his own head. It's easy to remember that the groin is the halfway point of the ideally proportioned height. The total height of a woman in ideal proportions is shorter than a man's by about half a head, but her total height still is eight times the height of her head. The ideal width proportions of a woman also would reflect more feminine characteristics: narrower shoulders and waist and wider hips.

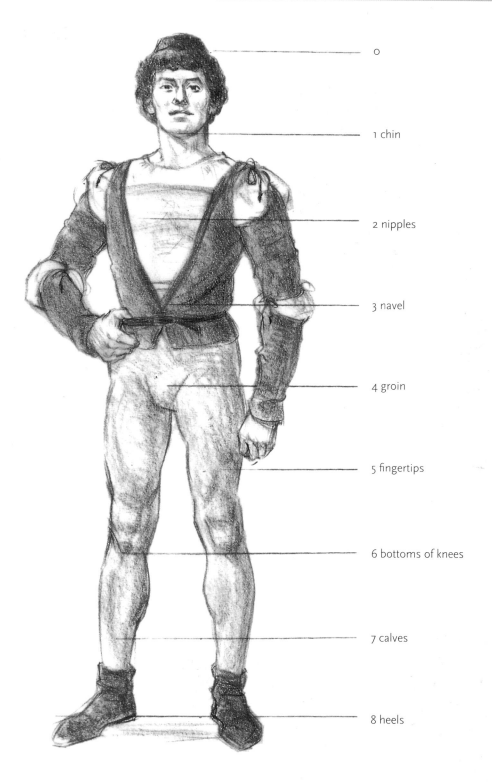

0

1 chin

2 nipples

3 navel

4 groin

5 fingertips

6 bottoms of knees

7 calves

8 heels

DEVELOPING A SENSE OF PROPORTION

To develop a good sense of proportion, spend time drawing figures from head to toe. Make it a practice to draw the entire figure in poses of seven minutes or less. If you're making a consistent mistake, you'll notice the pattern. Once you're aware of the problem, you can correct it as you go, training yourself to draw proportion correctly.

Harmonious Proportions
Compare this figure to those below, whose proportions are off.

Head Too Large
Artists often draw the head too large and then don't have room to draw the rest of the body. If you make this mistake often, draw an eight-head scale on the side of your paper so you can follow it as you draw.

Figure Grows
If the head's size is OK, but the figure seems to grow as you draw, just remember to refer frequently to the head and its size as you draw the rest of the body.

Idiosyncrasy
If you commonly make a mistake, such as drawing legs too short, simply overcompensate by drawing the legs too long. Eventually, you'll find a good balance.

DRAWING VARIED BODY TYPES

Essential to drawing a person is forming an opinion about whom you intend to draw. You can choose to depict not only certain emotional qualities, but also certain proportions and body types. Whether you are drawing from models or evolving characters from your imagination, figures whose proportions deviate from the ideal add reality, interest, contrast and unique elements to your pictures. When drawing people from your imagination, you obviously can visualize their characteristics. When drawing from a model, though, you also have choices. You can accept a person's attitude, expression and build as is. You can exaggerate any or all of these elements, or you can use your knowledge of standard proportions to completely change a model's build and proportions to what you want to draw.

Relate the Body to Ideal Proportions
For each figure you draw, compare these factors to the ideal proportions on page 35:

- figure's height, compared to the average
- total number of head measurements that make up the height, compared to the ideal eight-head scale
- variations within the figure's scale; rather than dividing into even sections, is a figure shorter from shoulder to hips with longer-than-average legs?
- proportion of general width of the body; is it more slender or broader than the ideal proportions?
- varied widths within the general shape; is a figure broad in the rib cage and comparatively slender in the hips?

1   2   3   4

Relate the Body Type to the Design
Use the design possibilities inherent in extreme body types. Mentally classifying body types helps me recognize them instantly. Drawing 1 reminds me of a beanpole, drawing 2 an egg, drawing 3 a pear and drawing 4 an hourglass.

Seeing and Drawing Perspective

In most natural positions, different parts of people's bodies are going in different directions, some heading away and some coming toward you. You view these parts in perspective. If you're looking up at a figure or looking down at one, you're seeing it in perspective. You could scientifically project every part of a figure in true perspective. But to best communicate what you want the viewer to see, you can not only use but also manipulate the visual effects of perspective, such as unusual relationships, foreshortening, wraparounds and overlapping forms. You'll learn more about drawing these effects in Part 3.

Unusual Relationships

When looking at a figure or one of its parts in perspective, the relationship between two body parts may be different than when viewing the figure at eye level.

Foreshortening

Things of equal size diminish with distance. The closer you are to a figure when you draw it, the more extreme is the effect of perspective. If a part of a figure goes away from or comes toward the viewer, it will appear shorter, or foreshortened, than if each part of the form were the same distance from the viewer.

Wraparounds

To make it clear that the viewer is seeing the figure or its parts in perspective, look for overlapping forms and how elements wrap around forms.

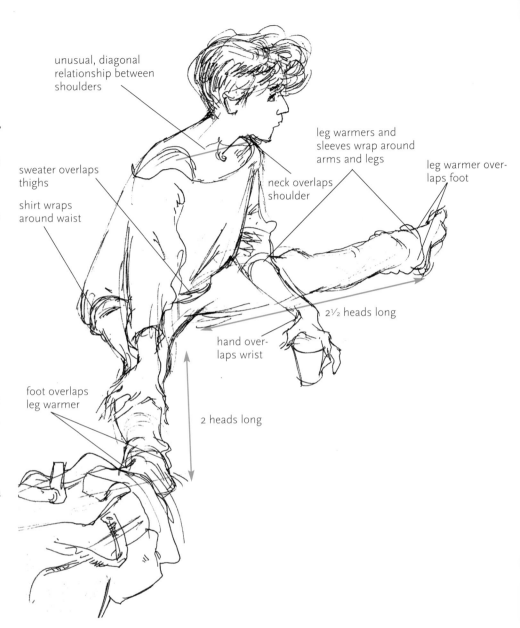

unusual, diagonal relationship between shoulders

sweater overlaps thighs

shirt wraps around waist

leg warmers and sleeves wrap around arms and legs

neck overlaps shoulder

leg warmer overlaps foot

2½ heads long

hand overlaps wrist

foot overlaps leg warmer

2 heads long

Effects of Perspective

While sketching a ballet class, I sat near this dancer as she took a break. Her position exhibited extreme perspective, which was made more extreme as I viewed her from above. Her outstretched legs, a position that would be uncomfortable for most people, also exhibited perspective, one coming toward me and the other heading away. Notice the unusual relationships: a line between her level shoulders looks diagonal in this perspective, and her chin appears lower than her left shoulder.

Though her legs are equal in length, about four heads long according to standard proportions, her left leg seems to be two and a half heads long and her right about two heads long when viewed in perspective. Use anything that wraps around a part of the body to communicate that the part is foreshortened, not merely short. Notice how the cuffs of the dancer's leg warmers wrap around her ankles. The type and degree of the curve that wraps around each leg shows the direction that leg is facing and indicates that it is seen in perspective. The dotted lines complete the ellipses around her figure. To further indicate your unusual viewpoint, take advantage of any form that overlaps another, such as her neck overlapping her shoulder near her chin.

ACCEPTING RELATIONSHIPS

I f you were an artist from Mars drawing the earthling at right, you'd accept that his nose is below his shoulder and his hand is as big as his head. As artists on Earth, we must learn to perceive and accept relationships that appear strange. To accept these relationships in daily life and to draw them are two separate things. We have become used to looking at people in scenes in perspective, but our brains do not accept that one arm seems shorter than the other. To draw in perspective, you have to break your brain of the habit of seeing like a nonartist and train it to see as an artist does.

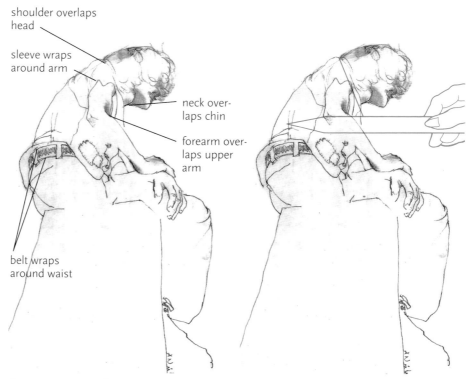

shoulder overlaps head

sleeve wraps around arm

neck over-laps chin

forearm over-laps upper arm

belt wraps around waist

Extreme Perspective
Tony Neila drew this twenty-minute drawing of a fellow student who was sitting high above him. Notice the many unusual relationships. His chin actually appears below the near shoulder. His elbow is only a little lower than his chin because of the drastic foreshortening of his upper arm. Notice the extreme curve of the figure's belt as it wraps around his waist and the areas where forms overlap forms. These occurrences enhance the extreme perspective and make it believable to the eye.

Seeing Unusual Relationships
When you see a person in extreme perspective, finding a true horizontal for comparison is difficult. Holding your medium horizontally in front of your eyes creates a true horizontal. Then you can move your arm up and down, comparing any relationship you see to the horizontal medium. In this case, it helped Tony see the extremity of the relationship between the figure's shoulders, represented by a solid line. Raising the pencil to the figure's right shoulder also would help Tony realize that the figure's entire face actually appears to be below the shoulder.

Opposite View
Student David Mar drew this reclining figure while sitting near the figure's head. Perspective makes the features of the upper body look larger close to the viewer and smaller farther away. The artist enhanced the perspective even more by using more detail on the upper body, closest to the viewer. Notice how extreme the curves of the sleeves are as they wrap around each arm to enhance the perspective.

5

Value

Value refers to the lightness or darkness of a color. The value of values is that you can use them to direct attention to a part of a picture and to clarify a drawing. You can create mood through light and shadow. You can enhance form with values. You can strengthen or even establish a picture's composition and design with a value pattern.

Line and tone often work together. Drawing in tone alone makes you aware of masses, form and light. Drawing in line alone encourages you to look, judge and think before drawing. The knowledge you gain from drawing in line helps you make decisions about the edges of each area of tone. And supplementing line drawings with value can enhance them. As you go through this book, look for drawings in which I've either supplemented line with tone or used value to help tell a story.

Value Can Supplement Tone
To clarify masses and shapes, I added values to this line drawing of a Comanche father presenting his child to the world. The dark values that I used for his skin tone also made the picture stronger by creating impact with contrast.

DETERMINING TONAL VALUE

Use a real or mental value scale to decide what values to use. Before applying tone to a drawing, decide whether to draw a line drawing that will be supplemented with tone or to communicate the picture by tone alone. Decide what local value you'll apply to each part based on a value scale. Decide if you want to indicate light and shadow, how that will affect local values, and what degree of contrast you want between light and shadow.

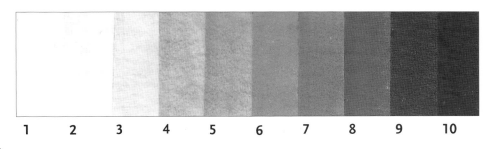

| 1 | 2 | 3 | 4 | 5 | 6 | 7 | 8 | 9 | 10 |

Value Scale
Determine the values you'll apply to each part of your drawing before you begin. This way you'll have the contrast you want between light and shadow, and you won't run out of values before you finish your drawing.

Assigning Values
This sailor makes an interesting subject because of the strong value contrasts. I used only value, not line, to communicate shapes. Both his uniform and the background are white, so I defined the shapes of the light parts of his suit with a little tone in the background. I used tone on the shaded parts of his uniform to define the edges of the other side. You can use contrast to define shapes within a figure, too. Notice how I used the shadow on his left thigh to define the shape of the light side of his right thigh.

If you're using tone to separate parts of a drawing with no strong light source, think of each part of a drawing as a family. Each family has a local value, and any tones within this family are close in value.

Changing Contrast

The drawing at near right is standing in medium light. You can see the value families I used to define each area. For the drawing at far right, I darkened each shadow to increase the contrast within each family. His suit now ranges between values 1 and 7 and his skin between 4 and 8. The new lighting makes him appear to be standing in hot sunlight.

1 - 4
suit

3 - 6
skin

9 - 10
shoes, hair, etc.

1 - 7
suit

4 - 8
skin

8 - 10
shoes, hair, etc.

Indicating a Light Source

I used no light source in the drawing at near right, so most of the contrast comes from local values. By adding some shadows, and thus increasing the range of values within each value family, I implied a light source for the drawing at far right.

1 - 3
baby, loin cloth

3 - 4
leggings

5 - 6
skin

10
hair

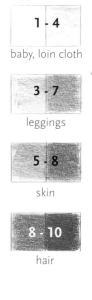

1 - 4
baby, loin cloth

3 - 7
leggings

5 - 8
skin

8 - 10
hair

LIGHT AND SHADOW REINFORCE FORM

O nce you know how the direction of your light source affects regular shapes and produces shadows and lit areas, you can transfer that knowledge to more complex figures. If you can picture a figure, such as a sailor, as a series of abstract forms, you can use light and shadows to better communicate his more complex form.

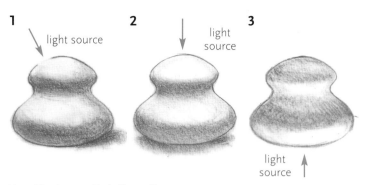

1 light source

2 light source

3 light source

Use Shadow to Reinforce Form

The same three-dimensional object, shaped like a squat bowling pin, appears in three different lighting situations above. Objects 1 and 2, lit from above, are shaded on the concave parts and lit on the convex parts. Object 3, lit from below, has shaded convex parts and lit concave parts. Object 1 also has a shadow on the right because the light source is shining from the left.

Look at Figures as Simple Forms

The light shining on this sailor is similar to the light shining on object 1 above except that it's shining from the right rather than the left. The forms of his figure that go away from the viewer, such as his left leg and his lower right arm, are in shadow, so I used tone to draw them. I didn't use any tone on the parts of his form that are receiving light, such as his right torso, upper right arm and the right side of his right thigh. Because his torso is twisted as he reaches forward with a mop, his shoulders also are lit and thus have no tone.

light source

Use Shadow to Reinforce Direction

I enhanced the directions and forms of this woman's general figure and its individual parts by applying shadow on the parts of her body that move forward, away from the viewer: her torso from her shoulder blades to her waist—indicating a forward thrust of her stomach—the area below her buttocks, her left arm from the elbow to the wrist, and the areas below the calves of her legs.

INDICATING CHANGES OF PLANE

Parts of a figure lie on a seemingly infinite number of planes, and each of those planes receives light from the light source differently. Use light and shadow to either represent a change of plane or to enhance it, making it more believable.

Words From the Master

Howard Pyle, one of the greatest picture-makers of the last century, referred to as the "father of American illustration," stressed to his students that halftones belonging to the light side should be painted lighter than they appear, while halftones belonging to shadow should be painted darker than they appear. Pyle's advice is as good today as it was one hundred years ago.

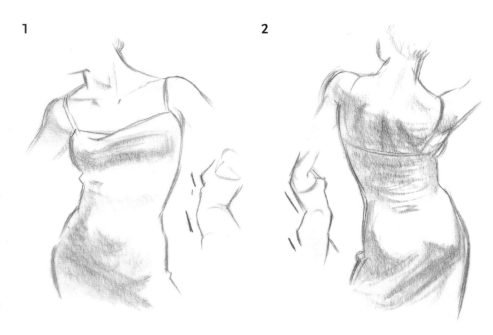

Use Tone to Indicate Changes of Plane

When drawing a figure from the front or back, also consider what it would look like from the side. Next to each of these drawings is a sketch of the same pose from the side. Drawing 1 is thrusting out her stomach. The lines along the side angle indicate the change of plane of her stomach and below her chest. Applying tone to these changes of plane enhances the definition of form. Notice the similar use of tone on drawing 2.

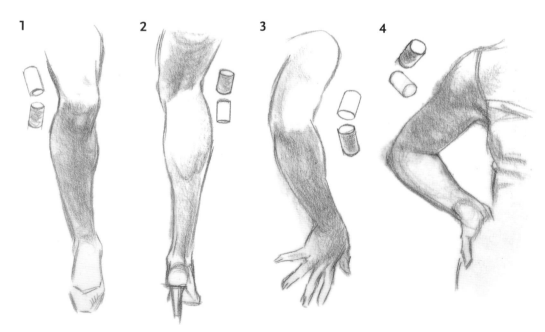

Use Value to Indicate Bends

Tone is particularly useful when parts of arms and legs are heading away from or coming toward you. When a light source shines from above: Tone below the knee (drawing 1) indicates a bend of the knee toward the viewer. Tone above the back of the knee (drawing 2) indicates a bend of the knee away from the viewer. Tone below the elbow (drawing 3) indicates a bend of the elbow toward the viewer, and tone above the elbow (drawing 4) indicates that the elbow is bending away from the viewer. The thumb overlapping her hip also enhances the impression that the arm is heading not just to the side but also behind her body.

USING SHADOW SHAPES

You can use shadow shapes to help define the parts of a figure receiving light. Really study the shapes of the shadows and the lit areas that you're drawing.

Holding Light With Shadow

Student Joel Yau used only one value to at once add tone to shadow shapes and define light shapes; he used no line at all. He ignored the structure of the folds and whether they had hard or soft edges, concentrating simply on the shapes.

DRAWING AIDES

ANY ANALYTICAL DEVICE THAT HELPS US OBSERVE, appreciate and empathize with the figures we draw is a drawing aide. Think of each aide as a finger. If you intertwine the ten fingers of your hands, you become conscious not of each finger but of your hands clasped together as a whole. So it is in a good drawing. A viewer is aware only of the effect of a drawing, not of the different parts that make it up. The hows—the aides, principles and techniques you use—intertwine to express the what—your opinion about the figure. Practice using the aides. They'll become your friends as you draw. You'll find that your ability to portray your figures in a storytelling manner will improve while the drawing process becomes easier, more effective and more enjoyable.

Stretch and Compression

Awareness and use of stretch and compression will help you bring life and movement to the figures you draw. In natural gestures, some areas of the body stretch and others compress. In dynamic gestures, stretches and compressions are obvious. Other times they may be barely perceptible. Whether obvious or subtle, take advantage of them. There is no better drawing aide for bringing vitality to your people than stretch and compression.

Stretch and compression occur in both large and small body masses, and they always work together. Whenever one part of the body stretches, the opposite side compresses. Empathize with gestures you see. When you can feel the stretches and compressions in your own bones and muscles, you're ready to observe and draw them on other people.

Stretch and Compression Work in Pairs
This North African dancer's torso, a large mass, stretches in two ways: toward the viewer and toward the right. Accordingly, the opposite sides, her back and left side, compress. Her wrists are smaller masses, but their stretches and compressions are vital to portray her expressive hand gestures. The wrists stretch on the inside of the arm toward the palm, and the tops of the wrists compress.

IN THE TORSO

The torso is composed of two masses, the chest and the pelvic area, which are connected by the spinal column. The spine is flexible, allowing the torso to move in all directions, leaning forward or backward, tilting side to side and twisting. Most natural positions combine these three movements.

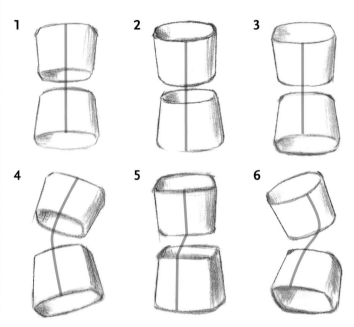

Imagine the Spinal Column

Think of a line drawn down the center of a figure's back as the spinal column. You can tell whether the form is leaning backward or forward depending on whether you can see the top or bottom of the form. And the imaginary line can indicate whether the form is leaning or twisting.

The entire torso can bend backward (drawing 1) or forward (drawing 2), or one part can bend forward and the other part back (drawing 3). Both parts can squeeze together on the same side (drawing 4). One part can twist (drawing 5) or, for the most complex combination, one part can bend forward, another part back, both parts squeezing together and twisting in opposite directions (drawing 6). Move your body to match these movements and feel how your torso and pelvis move in relation to each other. Also observe the bend of your spinal column in each position.

The Macaroni Principle

The macaroni principle is a mental trick that helps you recognize a torso's actions. Think of a torso as a giant, flexible piece of elbow macaroni. The concave part of the macaroni is compressed, and the convex part is stretched. Though this way of seeing actions is simplistic, it works. This model was in constant movement, flowing from one attitude into another. Looking for these simple shapes helped me recognize each position at a glance.

RECOGNIZING CONTRAPPOSTO IN THE TORSO

The word contrapposto describes the twisting action of a torso. It was a favorite gesture of Michelangelo. When a figure twists its torso, it often also stretches and compresses it. Train your mind to recognize contrapposto combined with stretch and compression. Once you recognize them, you can easily record what seemed like a complex gesture.

Stretch and Twist
The model's shoulders face forward while her pelvis faces 45 degrees away. Not only is her torso stretching toward the viewer, which means her back is compressing in, her torso also is twisting in contrapposto. This model and the others drawn on this page were moving. Because I could recognize contrapposto quickly, I was able to capture the essence of their gestures.

A Difficult View
To indicate stretch or compression toward or away from you, rather than to the side, look for any element that wraps partially around the figure, such as the lines of this model's thigh and torso that overlap on the compressed side.

Side Views Are Easy to Recognize
A side view shows a simple view of a forward stretch and backward compression.

IN THE NECK

The position of the head and neck can establish the attitude of an entire figure and hint at the person's emotions. Besides the angle of the head, look for any stretch and compression in the neck that can reinforce a gesture.

Graceful Indifference
The stretch of this woman's neck as she thrusts her head forward, upward and slightly away expresses a disdainful attitude.

Arrogance
As this man thrusts his head back and lifts his chin, the back of his neck compresses. At the same time, he gazes downward.

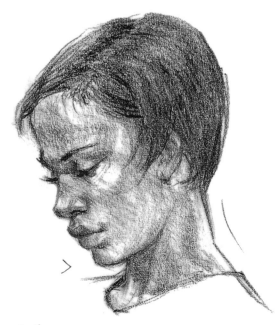

Concentration
This woman tilts her head downward, compressing the front of her neck. She also thrusts her body forward, amplifying the compression. Her lowered eyes express thought.

Pride and Contemplation
This man thrusts his head back, expressing pride, but the compression of his chin against his neck and the way he lowers his eyes add a feeling of contemplation.

In Legs and Arms

To appreciate stretch and compression in your figures' legs, feel them in your own body. Lunge forward, putting your weight on your bent right leg while stretching your left leg behind you.

On your left leg, feel the stretch on the front of your thigh and the corresponding compression of your buttock against the back of your leg. On your right leg, feel the stretch of your buttock and the upper part of the back of your leg and the corresponding compression of your lower torso against your thigh. You can do similar exercises to feel stretch and compression in your arms.

Running Stretches
This runner's torso stretches outward and forward, compressing his back. That stretch continues through his left leg, compressing the back of his leg against his buttock. The folds of his shorts reflect that compression. Although you can't see it, you can imagine the stretch from his buttock through the back of his right leg and the compression between his torso and the front of his right leg.

1

2

3

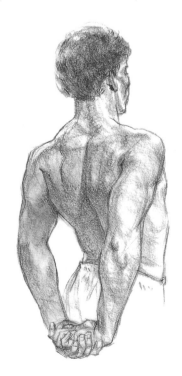

Stretch Your Arms
To feel the effects of stretch and compression in your arms, try these gestures. Cross an arm over your chest (drawing 1). With hands clasped, lift your arms high (drawing 2). Clasp your hands behind your back (drawing 3). In each of these poses, feel the stretch of the outer part of your arm as you press your inner arm against your body.

In Ankles and Wrists

Stretch and compression both occur whenever there is a change of direction at an ankle or wrist. These small elements contribute a great deal to the attitude or gesture you're trying to convey.

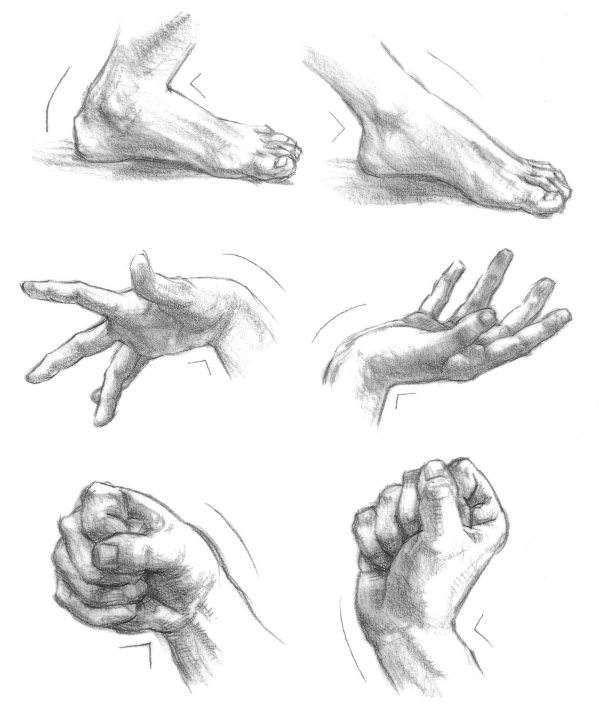

Sharp Bends
Stretch and compression usually occur naturally at the ankle, though the indications often are slight. The sharp bends of these ankles make the effect more obvious.

Avoid a Static, Straight Wrist
Each of these hands changes direction at the wrist drastically enough to make stretch and compression effects obvious. The degree of change of direction depends on the figure's gesture, but to make the gesture look natural, show some change, even if it's slight.

7

Wraparounds & Overlapping Forms

Any element that wraps wholly or partially around any section of the body is called a wraparound. A wraparound follows the contour of the form beneath it, revealing the volume and direction of the form below. Any element that overlaps part of the body or clothing is an overlapping form. Such elements that wrap around or overlap can be parts of clothing or the body. Often, elements overlap and wrap around forms at the same place.

Using these two drawing aides is the easiest and most effective way to bring three-dimensionality to your people, whether drawing in line or tone. It's also the simplest way to lend solidity to line drawings.

Drawing Aides Make a Big Difference
Look at the areas where this woman's clothing wraps around her body, such as the curved line where her bathing suit bottom curves around her stomach or the cross-contour lines of her top as they wrap around her upper body. Also notice areas where parts of her body overlap others. A line near her left armpit indicates where the flesh along the front of her arm overlaps the muscle that begins on the back of her shoulder.

USING WRAPAROUNDS AND OVERLAPPING FORMS

You can indicate so much form with just a single line, like those that indicate these figures' clothing and shoes. The way her bikini lies on her body and the way her body parts overlap or interact define the form and direction of her body and pose.

Recognizing Aides
During the few seconds the model held this pose, I looked for forms that wrapped around and overlapped other forms. Once I recognized them I could quickly establish the varying directions of her torso that were essential to communicating her gesture. The overlapping flesh at her waist and right upper arm suggest compressions, which also helped me establish direction and form.

Wrap Lines Around Forms
Clothing hangs straight down when it's on a hanger. But clothing takes on the form of the body wearing it and can help you communicate the form to viewers of your drawings. The lines of her bikini follow her contour, indicating the stretch of her torso and the thrust of her left hip. They also contribute to her three-dimensionality. Her left hand also wraps around or follows the contour of her hip. Even her shoes wrap around the forms of her feet.

Overlap One Form Over Another
Notice the many small but useful places where one part of her body overlaps another, enhancing form and suggesting direction. Simple lines can indicate these overlapping masses.

ON THE BODY

Perspective affects the way clothing looks as it wraps around the body. Take any chance you get to study how clothing lies on figures from different viewpoints. Then use this knowledge to help you draw clothing that clearly indicates your figures' gestures and locations.

1

2

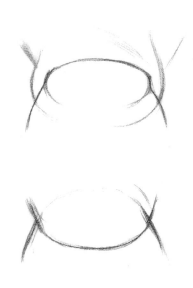

Show Direction With Overlapping Forms

Notice how this figure's clothes wrap around her body to indicate the directions of her forms. If she were standing straight up, the stripe on her shirt and the line between her shirt and her skirt would be straight. Instead they curve in different directions to indicate whether she is leaning forward or backward. The forms of her clothes also overlap each other to indicate which way she is leaning. Also notice the appearance of her neckline as she changes position.

Be Aware of Perspective

As this woman leans backward (drawing 1), the line of her hips overlaps the line of her blouse. Leaning forward (drawing 2), her blouse overlaps her skirt and hips. The overlapping forms that you see at the corners, though small, communicate so much.

1   **2**

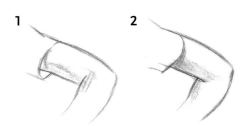

Identify the Form First

Before drawing any lines that wrap around a form, locate what is essential to a gesture. When this figure takes different postures, the action of his torso and the position of his shoulders also differ. It's tempting to use aides like wraparounds and overlapping forms before having the information you need to draw them effectively. Don't guess. Gather what information you can before drawing. Find the form; then have fun drawing the wraparound!

Small Details Make a Big Difference

The placement of one short line at the bend of the arm can communicate such a different image. The forearm in drawing 1 is directed slightly forward, and the forearm in drawing 2 is directed backward. Notice how I overlapped the line of the lower arm over the upper arm in drawing 1. When I continued the line of the upper arm in drawing 2 to overlap the lower arm, the arm seems to move away from the viewer. The way the sleeves wrap around the arms also reinforces the different viewpoints.

Finish Wraparounds

As you draw a line that wraps around a contour, make sure you draw the ends of the line so that if the line would continue behind the form, it would wrap around the form in a circle or ellipse. Your forms lose solidity if you carelessly extend lines that should wrap around a form. To indicate the form of the leg, the line of the sock that wraps around it should curve upward before it curves behind the leg.

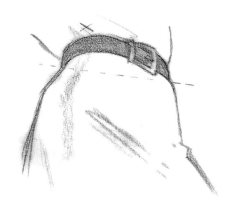

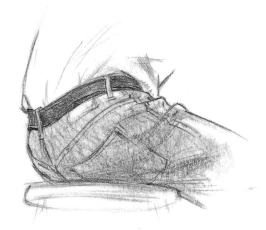

Define Specific Forms

In a quick sketch, don't worry about drawing every detail of a cross-contour line. It's enough to describe just a figure's general form and direction with wraparounds. When drawing a longer pose, you can add subtleties to the curves. This tank top's strap wraps around his shoulder, suggesting the curve of the clavicle.

Notice Essential Factors

Ask yourself, "How do the corners of her belt relate to one another; is one higher than the other? Where does the line of the belt change to reflect a change of direction or plane? What do the overlapping forms at the corners of her belt tell me about the gesture?" A line drawn between the corners of this woman's belt is horizontal. Her belt seems flatter as it wraps around her stomach. Notice the high point where the wraparound changes direction to begin wrapping around her side. The way the skirt and blouse overlap at the corners of the belt reinforces the thrust of the figure's hip toward the viewer.

Work Around Other Factors

You can still use lines that wrap around even if other factors seem to interfere. This rancher is leaning forward, causing his lower back to stretch and pull down the back of his jeans and belt. I indicated this downward pull and then emphasized the upward curve of the belt to compensate.

ON THE HEAD AND HANDS

I n addition to making the head seem three-dimensional, wraparounds and overlapping forms tell a viewer a lot about the tilt and direction of the figure's head.

Facial Features Play a Part
Notice the features that tend to wrap around the face: the eyebrows, eyes and lips. Parts of the eyes, nose and lips overlap other forms, depending on the tilt of the head.

Capturing Attitude From the Beginning
Capturing the main overlapping forms helps to indicate attitude almost as much as details do. Compare the feeling of the quick indications to the more detailed sketches. Both capture the heads' attitudes, but the quick sketches indicate the same feeling as the detailed drawings do.

On Fingers
Think of the fingers on this hand as a series of forms. The segments of each finger overlap each other and partially wrap around the inside of each finger, bringing out their forms and showing the direction of each joint. Another way to think about this concept: The overlapping forms are coming toward the viewer and the overlapped forms are heading away.

On Nails
Like clothing around parts of a figure, the lines of a fingernail or toenail wrap around the finger or toe. Notice how perspective affects the shape of a fingernail when seen from different views.

ON THE ENTIRE FIGURE

Overlapping forms and wraparounds appear on areas as large as the torso and as small as fingers. Both are important for communicating a three-dimensional figure.

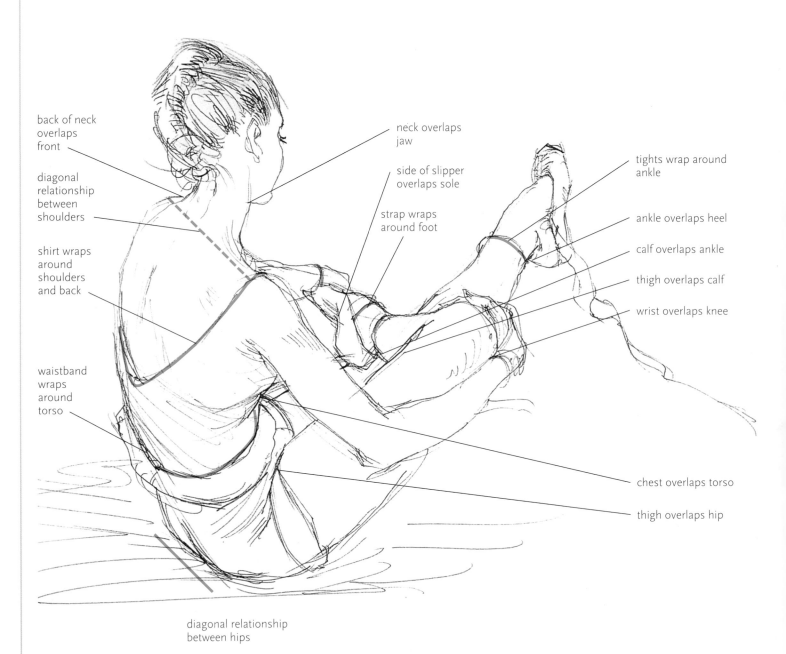

back of neck overlaps front

diagonal relationship between shoulders

shirt wraps around shoulders and back

waistband wraps around torso

neck overlaps jaw

side of slipper overlaps sole

strap wraps around foot

tights wrap around ankle

ankle overlaps heel

calf overlaps ankle

thigh overlaps calf

wrist overlaps knee

chest overlaps torso

thigh overlaps hip

diagonal relationship between hips

Bring It All Together

The rolled waistband immediately establishes our downward view as it wraps around her waist. The indication of the downward view is supported by many smaller lines that wrap around the dancer's figure and its parts. Notice that wraparounds and overlapping forms often occur at the same place.

8

Relationships

The term relationship, in figure drawing, refers to an imaginary straight line drawn directly from one body part to another. Seeing relationships accurately, such as those between the body and the ground and between main parts of the body, enables you to add believability to the way a person is standing, whether relaxed, dejected, determined or proud. Once you can observe relationships accurately, you also can learn when and how to exaggerate them to add vitality to your drawings and better express your opinion about a figure's gesture.

Making a Figure Look Natural
Imagine straight lines running through parts of this figure: from his head to the ground, between his shoulders, between his hips and between the heels of his feet. These lines all represent relationships. Even imaginary lines drawn between the heel and toes of each foot are relationships. I had to see all of these relationships accurately to make his stance natural and convincing.

Factual and Apparent Relationships

When looking at a figure, look for two kinds of relationships. Factual relationships are those that exist in reality. Apparent relationships are relationships as seen in perspective. For instance, if a man is standing straight, his shoulders are level. This straight line is the factual relationship. When viewed from above or below, the shoulders still are level, but a line drawn between them appears diagonal. This diagonal is the apparent relationship.

The factual relationship is what you want to communicate, what you want the reader to understand from your drawing. The apparent relationship is what you actually see. Looking at a figure from different views doesn't alter the factual relationship, but it does alter the apparent one.

Factual Relationships
The primary factual relationships of this man are that he has level shoulders and level hips. His feet are apart with weight distributed equally on both legs. Each horizontal line represents a factual relationship.

Apparent Relationships
Compare this view of a figure at a three-quarter view to the front view at left. His shoulders no longer appear to be on a horizontal line. The factual relationship—level shoulders—has not changed, but the apparent relationship has changed from straight to diagonal.

Determining the Direction and Slant
The direction of a diagonal relationship depends on the viewer's eye level. The viewer views this figure from above. If viewing him from below, the lines that indicate apparent relationships would slant the other direction. Two factors affect how extreme the slant of the relationship is. The farther the viewpoint is above or below eye level and the closer the viewer is to the figure, the more extreme is the slant.

Adjusting Relationships
You can revise a factual relationship to conform to the image you want to communicate. This model's relaxed head and torso weren't as authoritative as I wanted them to be in my drawing. I changed the relationship between the back of his head and his back so they align. This one adjustment changed the figure's entire attitude.

Primary relationships, those between main parts of the body, are essential to establishing a gesture. Secondary relationships, such as the angle of the head, the direction of the feet and the relationship of the wrists to the hips, can change without affecting the general attitude. Secondary relationships are important in conveying emotion and character.

Before drawing an upright pose, observe how the figure's weight is distributed—equally on both legs, all on one leg or more on one leg than the other? Imagine a vertical line from the head to the ground. If the weight is on one leg, the head will align with the foot bearing the weight. The relationship of the alignment of the head to the ground establishes the distribution of weight.

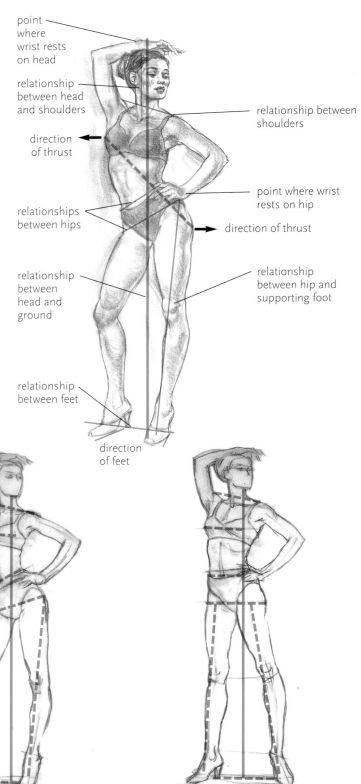

point where wrist rests on head

relationship between head and shoulders

relationship between shoulders

direction of thrust

point where wrist rests on hip

direction of thrust

relationships between hips

relationship between head and ground

relationship between hip and supporting foot

relationship between feet

direction of feet

Typical Relationships

Most of these relationships are primary. The relationships between her right wrist and the top of her head, her left wrist and her hip, and the direction of her feet are secondary. Notice that her chest is thrusting in one direction and her left hip is thrusting in the opposite direction. A line drawn between these thrusts represents another type of relationship.

Uneven Weight Distribution

This figure bears her weight on one leg. Notice that her head aligns with the supporting foot. The line from her hip to that foot heads diagonally inward.

Even Weight Distribution

Now she's bearing her weight equally on both feet, so her head aligns with a point halfway between them (in perspective). The line from each hip to each foot heads outward diagonally.

Weight Distribution

To draw a balanced figure, distribute its mass evenly over a central point, using relationships to describe the center of gravity and range of distribution.

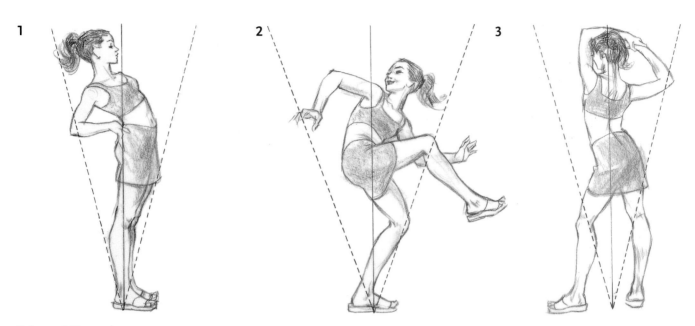

1　**2**　**3**

Balanced Figures

In each of this girl's gestures, her weight is equally distributed on both sides of a vertical line extending from her center of gravity to her feet. Drawing 1's torso on the right side of her center of gravity balances her arms, shoulders and head on the left. Drawing 2 has two legs and an arm on the right side of the center line and only one arm on the left. But her torso, a larger mass, also lies on the left side, balancing her weight. Drawing 3 has an arm and a leg on each side of her center of gravity, but she is leaning all of her weight on her right leg. To balance that weight, her torso thrusts to the left of the center of gravity.

Unbalanced Figures

Each group of lines, indicating the distribution of weight of each figure, leans in the direction of the figure's movement. Unbalanced poses give your figures a sense of movement, which you can amplify with small changes, such as the runner's lifted left heel. Though models have to be in balance to pose, you can deliberately make a model appear unbalanced by changing the distribution of weight.

STATIC AND DYNAMIC RELATIONSHIPS

The line that represents a relationship can be static (close to horizontal or vertical) or dynamic (diagonal). Static relationships lend dignity and repose to a figure. Dynamic relationships bring action and vitality to a figure. The more extreme the diagonal, the more energetic the gesture becomes.

In some gestures, different parts of the body thrust, or push, in different directions. The diagonal relationship between thrusts of the body is an important one to recognize because like all dynamic relationships it adds energy to a drawing.

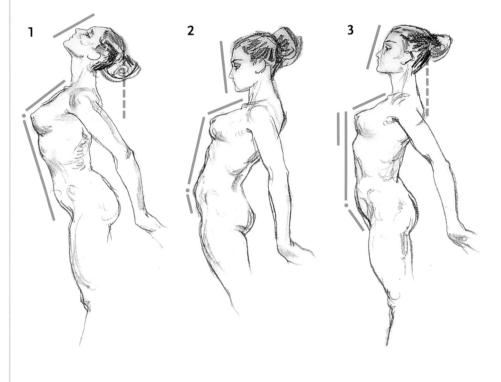

Thrusts and Directions

Observe the place on each of these three figures where thrust is greatest. Also observe the spot where the thrust stops and the body changes direction. Drawing 1 thrusts her chest forward and her torso changes direction below her chest. An imaginary line between her chest and her buttocks forms a strong dynamic relationship. The line from her chest to her neck and the line from her chin to the top of her head also are diagonal, conveying vitality.

Drawing 2 thrusts her stomach forward, forming a long diagonal that changes direction at her stomach. Her shoulder blades and head thrust backward, in the opposite direction. The relationship between her stomach and her shoulder blades is dynamic, though in an opposite direction from drawing 1. Drawing 3 thrusts out her entire torso from her chest down to her stomach. This action produces a more static relationship than those in drawings 1 and 2.

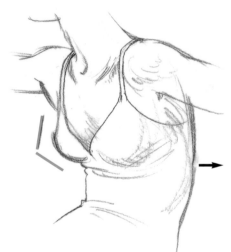

Direction of Chest

When drawing profiles, many artists automatically draw a traditional shape to indicate a woman's breast. Such a hasty indication can throw off an entire drawing. Different thrusts of the torso create entirely different directions and diagonals of the chest. Really observe forms and masses before drawing them. Don't make any assumptions.

Establish essential parts of the body. Then draw the parts that relate to it.

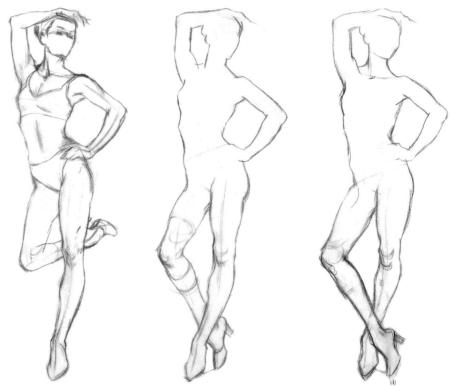

Arms on a Torso
When arms rest on a torso, locate the supporting part of the torso before drawing the arms. This woman thrusts out her chest in defiance, folding her arms across her chest, rather than slumping her chest under folded arms. I made sure to locate her chest before drawing the arms resting over it.

Supporting Leg
When your figure is resting all her weight on one leg, always relate the other leg to this supporting leg, locating the supporting leg first. To modify or improve the composition or gesture, you can make slight changes to the free leg, but not to a supporting leg. Notice that although the free leg changes in each of these drawings, the supporting leg remains the same. Try standing with all your weight on one leg and experimenting with the many different ways you can move your other leg.

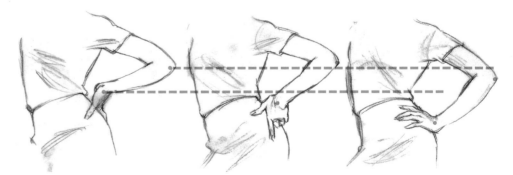

Hand on Hip
Always locate a hip before drawing a hand that rests on it. In this gesture, the woman changed the placement of her hand on her hip, a secondary relationship, without changing the relationship between the parts of her torso. Before I drew the diagonals of the arm, I needed to know her hip's location and then the wrist's relationship to it. Note the different elbow and wrist locations. The relationship between her hip and her wrist differs in each drawing. This changes the diagonal between her shoulder and elbow. Had I drawn her arm first, I wouldn't have been able to draw her hand resting naturally on her hip.

SQUEEZE POSE

The relationship between parts of the torso is an important primary relationship. One torso pose is so common that I've given it a name: the squeeze pose. It occurs when a shoulder and hip on the same side squeeze together, like an accordion. The other side of the body exhibits a high shoulder and low hip. The squeeze pose is most obvious from the front, but once you learn to recognize it, you'll know what signs to look for from any angle.

1 **2**

Vary the Degree to Vary the Attitude
When subtle, the squeeze pose can indicate a relaxed attitude (drawing 1). When extreme, the attitude changes. In drawing 2, the attitude is a fashion-like pose.

Recognizing It From the Side
It's difficult to recognize the diagonal relationship between shoulders and between hips from the side. Look for other clues to locate these key relationships. The way this dancer's clothes wrap around her waist imply that her right hip is higher than her left hip. The slightest hint of her left shoulder in drawing 1 is enough to place it and thus indicate its diagonal relationship with the other shoulder. In drawing 2, the fact that her right arm bends from the body at a low point also indicates that the right shoulder sits low. The best way to observe all key relationships is to walk around a figure until you gain enough experience to recognize them.

1 **2**

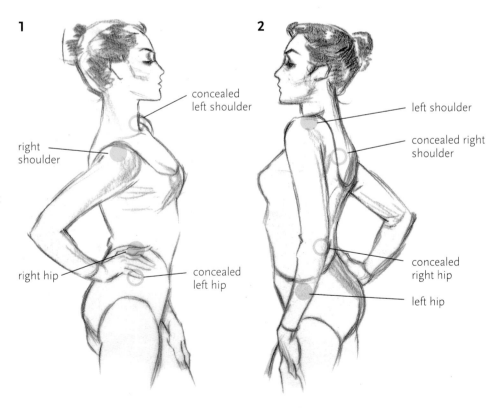

right shoulder

concealed left shoulder

right hip

concealed left hip

left shoulder

concealed right shoulder

concealed right hip

left hip

COMPLEX RELATIONSHIPS

The more complex a pose, the greater the number of key relationships to look for.

Grounding

To make standing figures believable in perspective, you've learned to observe primary relationships between the figure, the figure's feet and the ground. When a figure has multiple points of contact with the ground, though, you must also note the relationship between each of these elements.

Use an Imaginary Grid

Visualize a grid so you can cross-reference the interrelating parts of the body. You also can hold a pencil vertically or horizontally to help you see the relationships between various parts of the body.

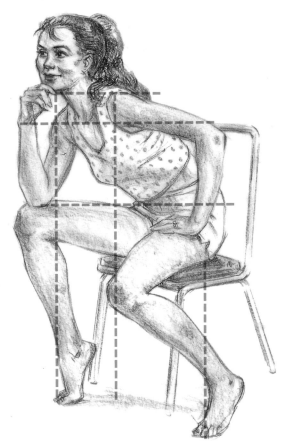

HEAD, NECK AND SHOULDER RELATIONSHIPS

The attitude of the head can be the key to an entire figure drawing. As soon as you draw the gesture of the head, you begin expressing your opinion about a figure. So begin direct drawings with the head. Because the face is the most difficult part to draw, it's easier to relate the rest of the figure to the head in location and proportion than to tack a head and face onto a torso and neck. I've never encountered a student who could successfully draw a face and head after drawing the body when drawing directly.

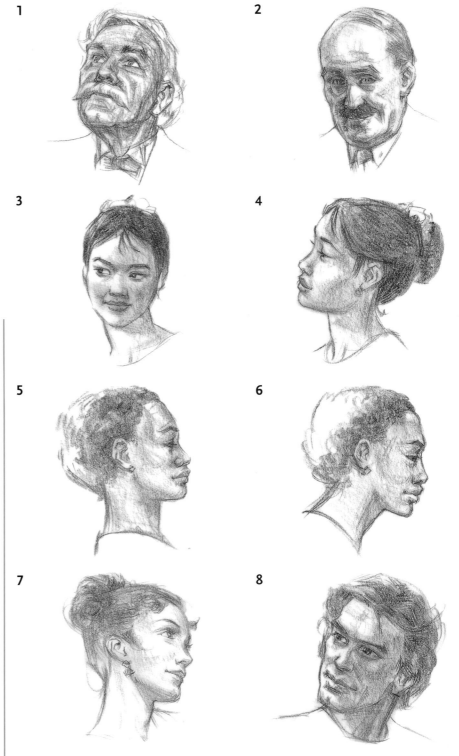

1

2

3

4

5

6

7

8

Relate the Head to the Shoulders
Relationships between the head and the shoulders are crucial when drawing figures leaning forward. To observe apparent relationships, visualize a grid, relating essential parts of the head and shoulders, such as the shoulder and chin.

Watch for These Three Head Actions
Look for any upward or downward tilt (drawings 1 and 2), any tilt to the side (drawings 3 and 4), any backward or forward thrust (drawings 5 and 6) or any combination of tilts and thrusts (drawings 7 and 8). These heads all show dramatically different attitudes.

FEET AND HAND RELATIONSHIPS

Primary relationships show a figure's basic action. Secondary relationships, though small, greatly enhance a gesture, lending it character and mood.

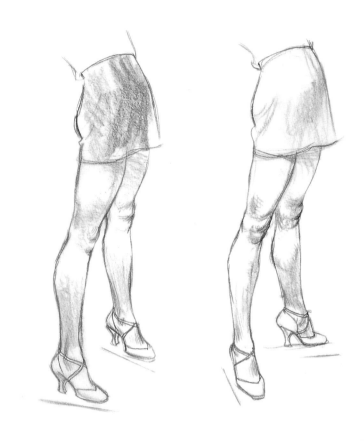

Convey Emotion

Except for the secondary relationships of this woman's feet, which also affect the knees, this figure's gesture is the same in both drawings. Her weight is distributed equally on both legs. She thrusts her pelvis forward similarly. But the feet do make a big difference; when her toes point inward, her attitude seems insecure, perhaps shy. When her toes point outward, it's confident and self-assured.

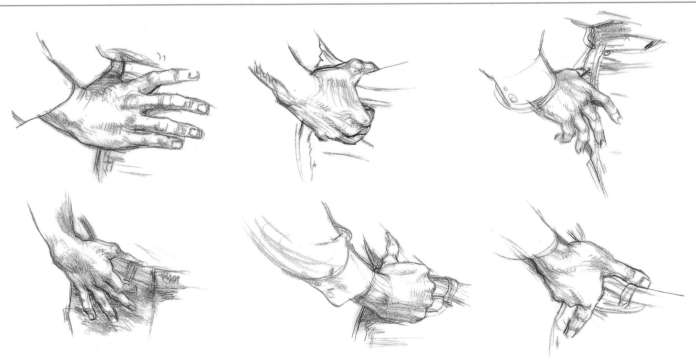

Hands on Hips Are Expressive

Once you've determined the location of a figure's hip, enjoy the many interesting ways a hand might rest there. The angle of the wrist and the relationship between the wrist and spot where it rests change in each of these drawings.

9

Rhythm and Continuity

Together, rhythm and continuity bring unity and beauty to your drawings. To understand and appreciate rhythm, imagine a flowing line that runs through the center of a mass. Think of rhythm as the flow through the center of a figure or part of the figure. To understand and appreciate continuity, look for continuous lines along the outside of a mass. Before drawing any figure, visualize the flow of its rhythm. Then, keep it in mind as you draw outside lines of continuity.

I probably stress rhythm and continuity to my students more than any other drawing aides. The invisible curved lines of rhythm bring natural feel to drawings. As you draw a figure part by part, be aware of the figure's whole. As you draw clothing, look for the continuity of body parts under the clothing.

Rhythm and Continuity Interrelate
Look for the invisible lines of rhythm through the figure and through her individual parts. Then look for the continuity of her figure's outside lines, even under clothing.

Understanding Rhythm

Some artists use the word "rhythm" to describe flows that zigzag from one side of the body to the other, establishing a rhythmic pattern of curves. However, many students misuse this form of rhythm by mistakenly merging a line of continuity—an outside edge of the body—with a line of continuity on the opposite side. Allowing an outside line to cross over the body and continue on the other side sacrifices the continuity of the *outside* edges and loses three-dimensionality. I pay attention to the pattern of curves that denote thrusting masses, but I use the word rhythm to describe the flow only through the body, never around it.

Different Ways to Look at Rhythm
The line in drawing 1 forms a zigzag rhythm, indicating the thrusts of different parts of the figure's body. The lines through drawing 2 indicate the flow, or direction, of parts of the body. Thinking of rhythm this way will help you draw more accurately without confusing lines of rhythm with the outside form of the figure.

What Causes Rhythms?
Rhythms are caused by a combination of three things: a figure's gesture, a figure's anatomy and the viewpoint. If one of these three factors changes, the entire rhythm changes. These legs, shown from the front (drawing 1), a ¾-view (drawing 2) and from the side (drawing 3), have the same anatomy and gesture: a locked knee. Though only your viewpoint has changed, the rhythm in each sketch is different. Memorize the rhythm and relationships of a side view of a locked knee (drawing 3). You'll draw it frequently.

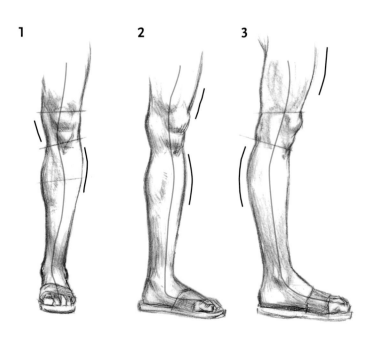

RECOGNIZING RHYTHM AND CONTINUITY

Think of a rhythm as a flexible wire going through the center of a mass. You can't see it, but you can imagine it.

To understand continuity, look for any continuous line along the outside of a mass. When clothing conceals the outside lines of the body, you have to look through the clothing, as if you had X-ray vision, to see these lines. Lines of continuity extend until you reach an overlapping form or a contrasting action of another part of the body. Look for continuity in stretches. As you draw stretches and other lines of continuity, draw the smaller curves that indicate anatomy, but always keep in mind the primary curve of the entire stretch.

Center Rhythm Lines
Notice the primary line of rhythm that extends all the way from the dancer's neck through the toes of her right foot. Another extends from her shoulder through her fingers.

Outside Continuity Lines
The outside lines of continuity on this dancer continue unseen under the bulges of her clothing and through her torso and right leg, behind the forward action of her left leg.

1

2

Finding Them Under Clothing
Establishing rhythm and continuity on the body are vital when drawing forms concealed by clothing. Analyze what the person is doing and look for clues to locate relating parts of the body. Lines of rhythm in drawing 1 tell us that this boy is thrusting his tummy forward and that his knees are locked. Notice the many places where continuity is suggested on the outside edges of (drawing 2) even though clothing protrudes from his body. Lines of continuity follow the boy's form rather than the form of his clothing. Finding these lines of continuity can help find his rhythm, especially under clothing.

IN THE FIGURE AND ITS PARTS

Y ou can apply the concept of rhythm to an entire figure and to its individual parts. Think of the rhythm of the entire figure before you start drawing, but make sure you apply rhythm to individual parts to make your figures look natural. Most gestures show multiple rhythms. Whether they are long from head to toe or short from elbow to wrist, all are important when indicating natural gestures.

1

2

Simple and Complex Rhythms

The essence of both of this woman's gestures is one long curve. The other rhythm lines show the specific rhythms of the individual parts of her body. In the simple gesture of drawing 1, the secondary lines of rhythm are similar to the primary one. In the more complex gesture of drawing 2, the rhythms of her right leg and left arm counter the rhythm of the long curve. Form both of these gestures with your own body, sensing the curves and contrasts.

See a Rhythm to Its End

This arm shows one long curve of rhythm until the wrist, at which it becomes a compound curve, branching out into different curves for the fingers. See each rhythm all the way to its end.

IN LEGS AND FEET

I cannot overemphasize the importance of using rhythm to draw legs. Sadly, I too often see drawings from "The Sausage School of Drawing," using ovals for the thighs and lower legs and circles for the knees. The importance of rhythm extends from the legs to the feet.

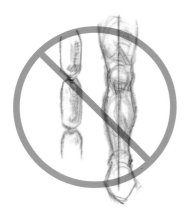

Avoid Sausage Drawing
Drawings that use sausage shapes for legs lack rhythm and look unnatural.

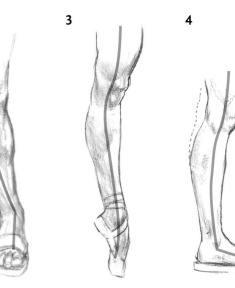

1 2 3 4

Look Until You Find Rhythm
Drawing 1 shows a a locked knee and the resulting typical shallow, reverse-S rhythm of the leg. Drawing 2 shows the rhythm of a leg slightly bent at the knee. If you can't find the rhythm as you look at a subject, move your head until you find a line of rhythm. Your drawings will look more natural and better communicate your gestures.

Drawing Locked Knees
When drawing locked knees from the side (drawing 3), draw the front of the leg first, making sure to thrust back the lower part of the knee. Then relate the back of the leg to the front. If you were to start with the back of the leg, you'd probably draw the leg in drawing 4, which does not indicate a locked knee. The back of the knee is pushed in, indicating a flexed leg instead. The position of the foot has no bearing on the rhythm of the knee, only on the rhythm through the ankle.

1 2

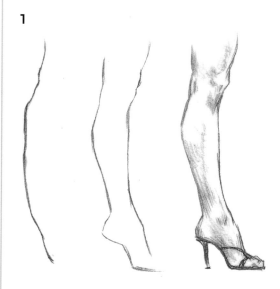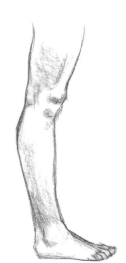

Drawing Locked Knees Step by Step
I drew the front line of continuity of each leg first. Then I drew the back line of continuity for each. I added details to each drawing in the final step. The front of the foot in drawing 1 stretches because the foot is in heels, so I extended the front line of continuity all the way to the curve toward the toes. In drawing 2, I indicated the stretch of the back of the ankle instead by extending the line of the back of the leg to the ground.

IN ARMS AND WRISTS

Always include the rhythm of the wrist and hand when determining the rhythm of an arm. If there is a stretch or change of direction of the wrist, continue drawing the line of that side of the arm to include it.

Relaxed Arm
As an arm, wrist and hand hang relaxed, their combined rhythm always forms a simple curve. The sleeve of a well-made jacket is actually curved this way to fit better. From the side, the wrist naturally changes direction slightly. Don't make the change in direction too drastic or the gesture will seem artificial.

Tense Arm
A strained arm has a different, and sometimes awkward, rhythm.

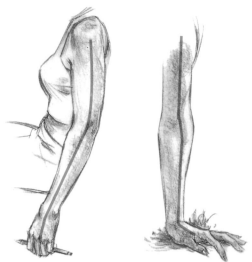

The Lower Arm Curves
Anatomy dictates that the rhythm of the lower part of the arm is a concave curve. Missing this rhythm creates a sausage arm.

Certain Views Emphasize the Curve
When the elbow of a bent arm faces you, the rhythm's curve is particularly pronounced.

Use Rhythm to Suggest Action
Changes of direction are useful in telling a story. Try raising and lowering your arms. Notice that your wrists lead the action, rising higher than the hand when raising the arm and falling lower when bringing the arm down. Each arm shows a gently curved line of rhythm until the wrist changes direction to indicate the direction of movement.

10

Using Drawing Aides Together

There are so many valuable drawing principles and aides to use and so much to observe that you may feel you don't know where to begin or how to put them together. The most important thing is to form your opinion about the figure and gesture you're drawing. Then use the drawing aides that best emphasize what you want to communicate about the person.

Logic, creativity, drawing principles (proportion, perspective and value) and drawing aides (stretch and compression, wraparounds and overlapping forms, relationships of forms, and rhythm and continuity) work together in the drawing process. Use a logical procedure to decide which aides and principles are essential to your opinion and which are less essential. Once you've made these decisions, you can draw more freely, decisively and quickly and you'll enjoy the drawing process.

Emphasizing Aides

Every drawing aide I've discussed in Part 3 appears in this drawing. Do you recognize them? I liked the stretch of the torso and the flow of rhythm throughout his body. I used overlapping forms to emphasize his muscular structure and wraparounds to enhance his solidity. Observing relationships helped me make him stand solidly on the ground.

AIDES WORK TOGETHER

Analyze this figure to see how the drawing aides work together. The formfitting clothing makes the drawing aides apparent as they apply to the figure. You'll learn how to draw figures under less defining types of clothing in Part four.

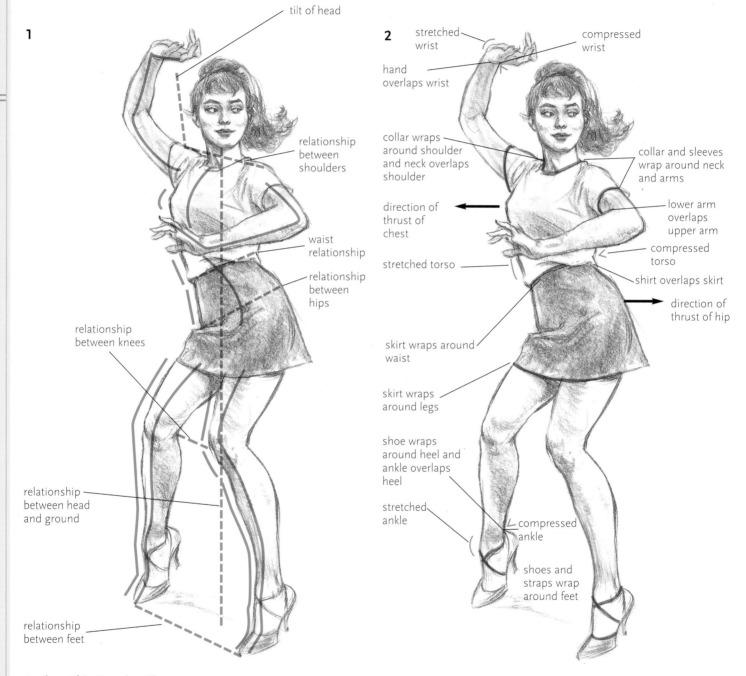

1

tilt of head

relationship between shoulders

waist relationship

relationship between hips

relationship between knees

relationship between head and ground

relationship between feet

2

stretched wrist

compressed wrist

hand overlaps wrist

collar wraps around shoulder and neck overlaps shoulder

collar and sleeves wrap around neck and arms

direction of thrust of chest

lower arm overlaps upper arm

compressed torso

stretched torso

shirt overlaps skirt

direction of thrust of hip

skirt wraps around waist

skirt wraps around legs

shoe wraps around heel and ankle overlaps heel

stretched ankle

compressed ankle

shoes and straps wrap around feet

Analyze This Dancing Figure

Notice the primary relationship between her head and the ground in drawing 1. Lines of rhythm run through her body and its forms, and lines of continuity run along the outside edges of her figure. Lines of rhythm pass through the intersecting lines of relationships.

Overlapping forms and wraparounds often occur at the same place. On drawing 2, the collar of her shirt wraps around her neck in the same place where her neckline overlaps her shoulder. The fold of her shirt overlaps the line that wraps around her waist. Notice that her rhythm lines bend toward stretches and away from compressions.

HOW TO PROCEED THROUGH A DRAWING

To decide when to draw what, appreciate and observe what a figure is doing. In a pose like the one at right, look for strong diagonal directions between parts of the body. You can emphasize these relationships in your drawing. The procedure you'll follow to draw a person differs with every gesture, but the principles you should consider apply to any pose.

Look for the most important factors about a person's attitude, draw them first, and relate the less important factors to them. For example, draw the most active side of a figure in order to place, or locate, it before drawing the other side. Use drawing aides to enhance the important factors and to provide solidity and spirit to your drawings.

Draw Stretches and Thrusts First

Draw a stretching side before drawing the compressed side. Draw the thrust before relating the opposite side to it. The drawing procedure is easy when the stretch and thrust are on the same side of the body, as in this figure. I first established the wonderful backward thrust of her head and neck. Then I could relate her shoulders and the rest of her body to this thrust. Next I drew the torso's stretched front. I located the area of most thrust, which is where the line of continuity changes direction. I then could relate her compressed back to the thrusting front.

After establishing the torso, I had enough information to relate the legs and arms to it and to draw the bikini. The compressed back created a diagonal change of direction in the body's rhythm. Following this path through the legs, I drew the stretched front of her leg before drawing the back. I contrasted the directions of her arm to the rhythmic curve of her body. Then I was able to enjoy drawing her bikini as it wrapped around her torso, making it solid and enhancing her gesture.

When Thrust and Stretch Occur on Opposite Sides

You should still establish thrusts and stretches before drawing their related sides, but when the thrust and stretch occur on opposite sides of the figure, you have to switch back and forth between them. To capture this figure's lovely squeeze pose, I again started with the head, neck and shoulders, making sure to show her left arm pressing against her head. From there I drew part of her stretched left side but quickly moved over to her right side to draw the sharp compression at her waist and the strong outward thrust of her hip. I then had enough information to draw her shirt and skirt band as they wrapped around her form to enhance it. Then I drew the arms and legs. I chose to draw the arms first because the left arm's contact with the head is so important to this gesture. Notice how the folds in her shirt emphasize the stretches and compressions in her torso.

Sherlock Holmes Principle

Sherlock Holmes would study the scene of the crime, then search for clues. In the same way, you should study the figure and consider which drawing aides would help convey the gesture. When part of the body is concealed by other parts of the body or by clothing, look for clues as Sherlock would. The most important parts of the body and action will direct you to the concealed parts. That's another reason to start a drawing with the parts most relevant to the gesture.

Draw Supporting Leg First

Locate the outer side of the right leg under the skirt, the figure's line of continuity, to help find the inner edge of the leg. To achieve continuity, I continued the line of the front of her leg, which almost faces away from the viewer, all the way down to the toes. Then I drew the back of the leg.

I drew the left leg next, again drawing the front first. The heel and details on a shoe can tell you much about the gesture of the feet, but they don't actually affect the structure of the gesture and can be left until last.

Hidden Supporting Leg

If the supporting leg is partially concealed by the working leg, don't be tempted to draw the working leg first. Draw what you can see of the supporting leg, relating it to the rest of the figure. Then draw the working leg, altering it as you need or want so it looks right with the supporting leg. Drawing the working leg first and relating the supporting leg usually causes the artist to miss the relationship of the supporting leg to the ground, which results in a figure that looks out of balance.

Search for Clues

Almost all the thrusting right side of this woman is hidden by her elbow and sleeve. I "looked through" her sleeve and arm to locate the hidden corner of her waistband where it wrapped around her thrusting right hip. Once I had found her waistband, I could relate her left side to her right, drawing the left side low and keeping her waist small.

DRAWING LEGS

To draw convincing legs that do what you want them to do, consider three factors before drawing: (1) Make a mental note of each leg's relationship to the other leg and to the body, (2) note the legs' rhythm, and (3) consider the figure's anatomy and each leg's build and proportion. As you observe more and more figures, you'll learn to associate typical relationships and rhythms with familiar gestures and poses and be able to draw legs convincingly.

Legs are wonderful to draw. Learn the anatomy of legs and characteristics that occur in typical gestures. Then you'll be able to understand the things that happen to legs in different circumstances.

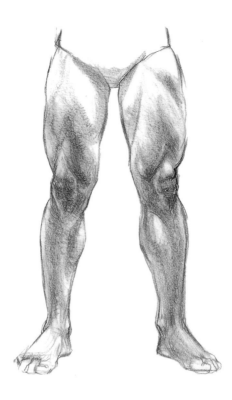

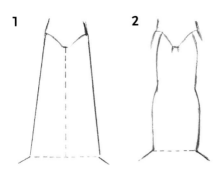

Make Mental Decisions

This figure's weight is distributed evenly on both legs. The knees are locked and the legs have heavy muscular development. First take some mental pictures. Observe the leg relationships (drawing 1). Because we're viewing the figure head-on, factual and apparent relationships are the same. Observe the rhythm of the legs (drawing 2). The locked knees and legs are turned out. Then, after taking time to study and appreciate the anatomy of his muscular build, you can draw.

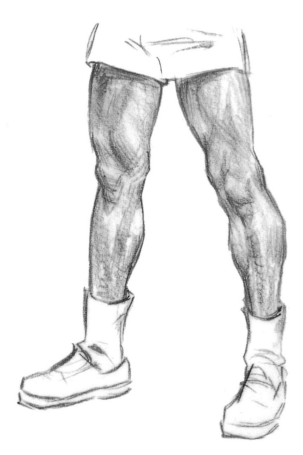

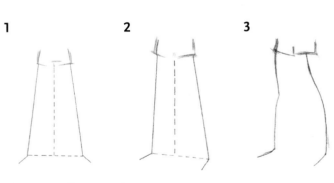

Observe Before Drawing

This figure also distributes its weight evenly on both legs. But at a ¾-view, the apparent relationship (drawing 2) and factual relationship (drawing 1) differ. From this view the rhythms of the legs (drawing 3) are no longer identical as they are in the figure at the top of the page. You see his right leg at a ¾-view and his left leg almost from the front.

Memorize Typical Occurrences

Memorize these diagonal relationships of the front view of a leg with a locked knee: above and below the knee, between the muscles in the middle of the lower leg, and between the bones of the ankle. Drawing 1 shows the legs of a baby, drawing 2 a five-year-old girl, drawing 3 an adult woman and drawing 4 an adult man. Proportions and muscular development can change, but these relationships will always stay the same. Note that the line of continuity along the inner side of the knee always changes direction toward the outer part of the leg. The side view of a locked knee on page 71 is another important typical relationship

1   **2**   **3**   **4**

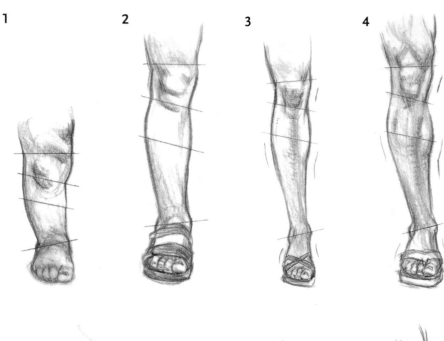

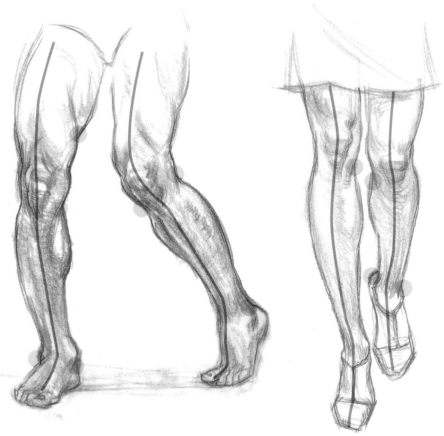

Visualize Wraparounds, Overlapping Forms and Rhythms

Even if you don't have clothing, such as a sock, to show lines that wrap around parts of the leg, visualize how such lines would look. When you see legs in perspective, visualizing these lines will help you see apparent relationships and rhythms (indicated by lines). Also look closely for small overlapping forms (indicated by circles) that will communicate the form, direction and muscular structure of the leg.

USING AIDES TO DRAW DIRECTLY

Drawing directly—drawing without a visible guide or an underdrawing—lends freshness and immediacy to any drawing, and it's the best way to draw quick poses and figures in motion. When drawing directly, you still use drawing aides, but the guide is in your head.

Draw models in poses of five to ten minutes to get used to recognizing and applying the drawing aides we've discussed in Part 3. With experience, you'll use them almost subconsciously.

Most beginning students have trouble seeing and drawing actions and relationships as strong as they actually are. Try exaggerating actions and making relationships more dynamic than they seem to be. Experienced artists often exaggerate actions simply to better communicate a gesture.

Changes in Rhythm Can Communicate Motion
Though there was little movement in this drummer's torso and legs, his hands beat at a furious tempo. I observed the alternating action of his arms, then relied on the rhythm of his arms and change of rhythm at his wrists to communicate the drumming. Neither of these drawings took longer than three minutes.

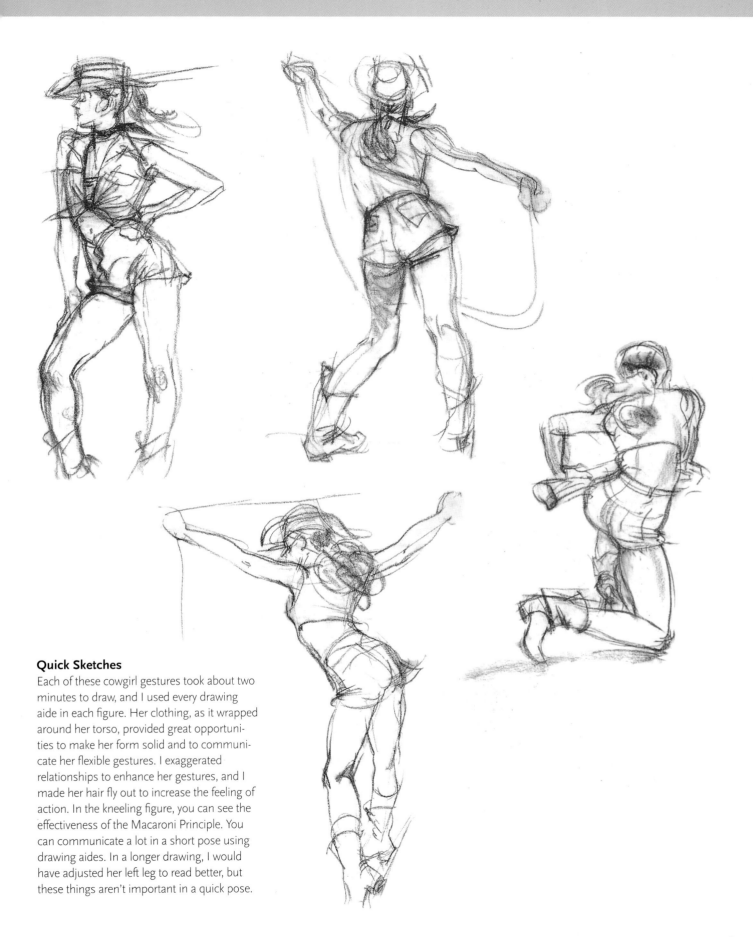

Quick Sketches

Each of these cowgirl gestures took about two minutes to draw, and I used every drawing aide in each figure. Her clothing, as it wrapped around her torso, provided great opportunities to make her form solid and to communicate her flexible gestures. I exaggerated relationships to enhance her gestures, and I made her hair fly out to increase the feeling of action. In the kneeling figure, you can see the effectiveness of the Macaroni Principle. You can communicate a lot in a short pose using drawing aides. In a longer drawing, I would have adjusted her left leg to read better, but these things aren't important in a quick pose.

4 DRAWING FOLDS

FOLDS AND DRAPERY CONFUSE MANY STUDENTS
and even intimidate some. Neither meticulously observing and copying
bumps and changes of value nor quickly sketching zigzagging lines to
approximate the folds allows you to interpret what you see. To be in charge of
the folds you draw on your people, you have to take time to learn about and
understand them.

Once you understand some basic principles, how to construct folds, how
they relate to the body, their usefulness in conveying information and ways to
draw them, you'll be able to draw folds and clothing on your people with
greater ease and conviction. Eventually your subconscious will respond to
your opinion, what you want to express, using this knowledge about folds to
communicate what you want. You will be able to manipulate folds to intensify action, emphasize three-dimensionality, improve composition and
design or tell a story. This is when the fun begins!

CHAPTER 11

What Folds Can Do for Your Drawings

Folds Show Form
Notice how these folds wrap around the form of this 1950s baseball player's figure as he stretches and twists.

When confronted with a model whose clothing is abundant with folds, you might wonder, "Should I try to copy the folds as I see them? Should I try to draw them all or eliminate some? Should I change some? If so, how?" The answers lie in knowing what folds can do for *you*. Assuming that you need not draw all the folds you see leaves you free to concentrate on the particular folds that are useful to your drawing. In this chapter, you'll see how you can use folds: to show form, intensify action or attitude, bring out the character of clothing and enhance design.

SHOWING FORM

Any fold or group of folds that wraps around a part of the body describes the form underneath. They also show direction and any stretch and compression of the body. As you draw a fold, be aware of the form you're indicating beneath it.

Wrapping Around Large Forms
Folds can wrap around large forms, such as the torso. Notice how wraparounds indicate the form of the figure beneath the clothing.

Wrapping Around Small Forms
You can also describe small forms, such as a boot wrapping around an ankle or a glove wrapping around fingers.

Showing Action and Attitude

Stretch and compression folds show action and enhance attitude. You'll find these in all but the most static gestures. The more flexible and active a gesture, the more stretch and compression folds you'll see. These folds usually curve, and the curves indicate the directions of the forms of the body beneath.

Stretch Folds

Stretch folds occur when tension between parts of the body causes a corresponding tension in clothing. Whenever a body stretches or twists, the clothing immediately over it also stretches. How visible the stretch fold is depends on the degree of the body's stretch and the style, fabric and fit of the clothing. Stretch folds fan out and curve as they progress from one point of tension to another.

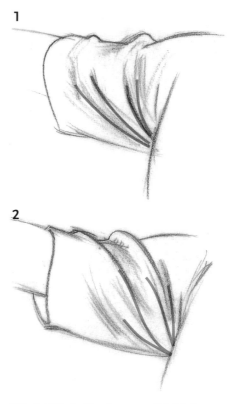

1

2

Tension Causes Fabric to Stretch
While wearing pants, sit down and feel the tension from under your buttocks toward your knees. This tension stretches the fabric of your pants, creating folds that fan out from your buttocks toward your knees and upper thighs.

What Affects the Curves of Folds?
Folds fan out from a source, which in these drawings is an area under and behind the arm. The way these folds fan out and the direction of the arm affect the shape of the curve. When the arm heads away from the viewer (drawing 1), the fanned out folds curve one way. When the arm comes toward the viewer (drawing 2), they curve the other way.

Compression Folds

Whenever one part of the body compresses or squeezes against another part, look for compression folds in the clothing directly over that part. Compression folds, which also can be called squeeze folds, almost always curve and, like stretch folds, describe the form and direction of the underlying form.

Feel These Actions

To anticipate where to find folds of compression, pose in these actions to create compression in your own body. As you feel the compressions on your body, study what they look like on the clothing in these drawings. Stretch your upper arm back (drawing 1). Feel it squeeze against your upper body. Sharply bend your arm (drawing 2). Feel the squeeze inside your elbow. Bend your leg sharply (drawing 3). Feel the squeeze behind your knee. Stand with one leg thrusting back (drawing 4). Feel the squeeze of your buttock against the back of your leg.

1

2

3

4
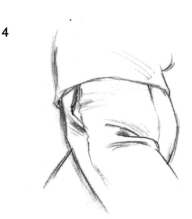

Small Folds Are Significant

Emphasizing small but significant areas of compression will help viewers empathize with the actions you're portraying. When you draw a foot stretched out (drawing 1), show the corresponding squeeze at the ankle's back. When the foot heads backward from the body (drawing 2), show the corresponding squeeze at the ankle's front.

1

2

STRETCH AND COMPRESSION WORK TOGETHER

On clothing, the stretch and compression folds that correspond to stretched and compressed areas of the body often merge and flow into one another. Take advantage of this natural occurrence to add fluidity to your drawings. Whenever you can, notice the clothes on models, friends, strangers, athletes and people in photographs. Look for similar patterns of folds in similar actions, noticing areas of stretch and compression in clothing over stretches and compressions of the body. Also notice how often stretch and compression folds flow into one another.

Merging Stretch and Compression Folds
The gesture of a batter as he ends his swing is a classic example of stretch and compression folds interacting and merging naturally. You can see stretch folds along the side of his right leg as he stretches it out in front of him. Compression folds appear where his left arm crosses over his chest, underneath his left buttock and between his torso and right thigh.

The areas where he twists merge the stretch and compression folds as they wrap around the forms. As he finishes his swing from left to right, he twists his body, merging the stretch folds from the front of his torso and the compression folds from his back as he leans back. As he pivots on his left foot, the stretch folds from his stretched thigh and the compression folds from his bent knee merge.

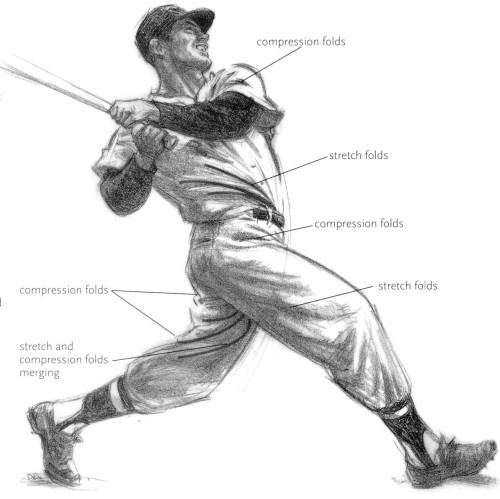

compression folds

stretch folds

compression folds

stretch folds

compression folds

stretch and compression folds merging

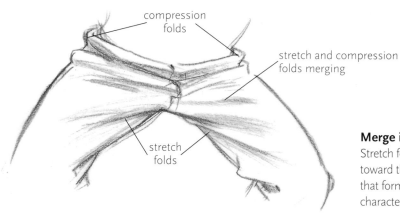

compression folds

stretch and compression folds merging

stretch folds

Merge in the Middle
Stretch folds traveling from the buttocks toward the knees merge with compressions that form at the tops of the thighs combining characteristics of both types.

Fold Patterns of the Squeeze Pose
You see folds like this in almost all squeeze poses. Study this figure and note where stretch folds and compression folds occur and where they work together. Then reference this knowledge whenever you draw squeeze poses.

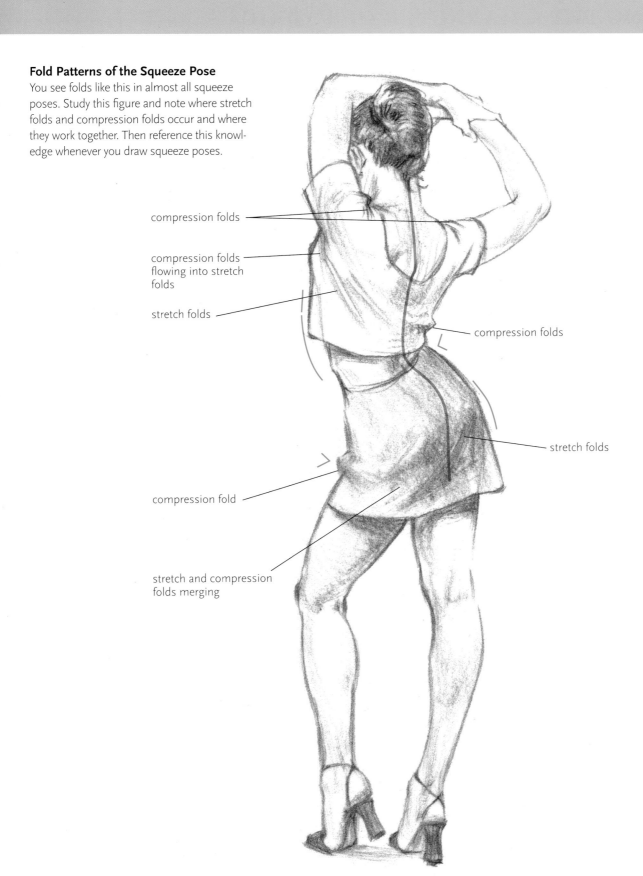

compression folds

compression folds flowing into stretch folds

stretch folds

compression folds

stretch folds

compression fold

stretch and compression folds merging

SHOWING THE CHARACTER OF FABRIC

The character of the clothing your figures wear is an important part of your visual descriptions of people. You can depict the character of a piece of clothing in detail in a careful three-dimensional rendering or suggest it in quick drawings. The fabric, condition, style and scale all lend character to clothing.

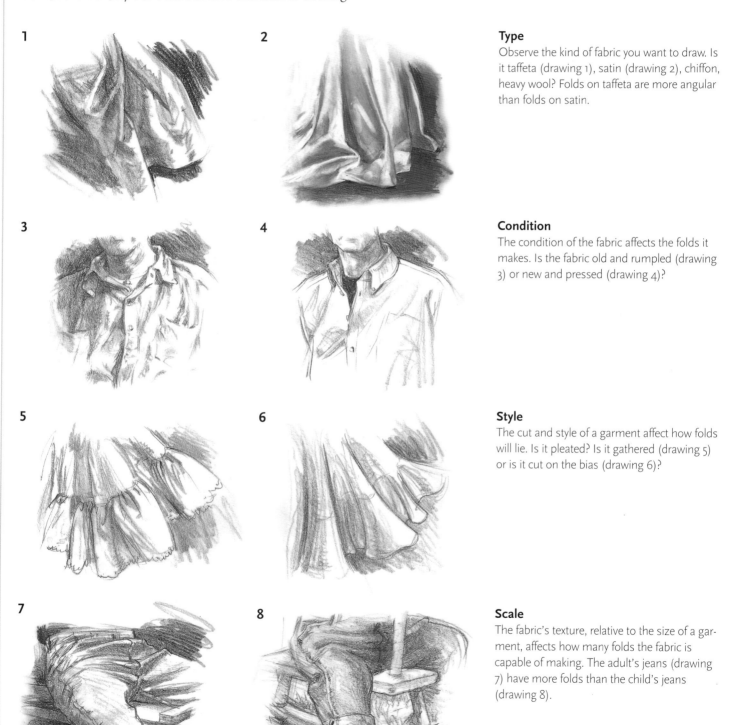

Type
Observe the kind of fabric you want to draw. Is it taffeta (drawing 1), satin (drawing 2), chiffon, heavy wool? Folds on taffeta are more angular than folds on satin.

Condition
The condition of the fabric affects the folds it makes. Is the fabric old and rumpled (drawing 3) or new and pressed (drawing 4)?

Style
The cut and style of a garment affect how folds will lie. Is it pleated? Is it gathered (drawing 5) or is it cut on the bias (drawing 6)?

Scale
The fabric's texture, relative to the size of a garment, affects how many folds the fabric is capable of making. The adult's jeans (drawing 7) have more folds than the child's jeans (drawing 8).

ENHANCING DESIGN

Folds on clothing can strengthen the design of an entire drawing. Try to make each area of folds or drapery pleasing in proportion to your overall drawing. Also try to arrange folds within each area to be pleasing in proportion to each other. Be selective. You can emphasize some folds and delete others. You can change their sizes and the spaces between them. You can change folds to vary the texture of a drawing, contrasting complex areas with simple areas. Controlling the value contrast within or between groups of folds also enables you to direct the viewer's eye to what you want them to see.

Stretch Folds
The stretch folds on this figure's right sleeve, pants and vest intensify his action. The curves of these folds contrast the straight lines on his figure. Also notice that one side of each sleeve is complex and the other simple. These decisions enhanced the total design of the figure.

Compression Folds
This hip-hop dancer's gestures stretched parts of his body and created stretch folds in his baggy clothing. I used compression folds to bring out the compression of his front torso, which brought out his form and intensified his action. The folds also improved the overall design of the figure by contrasting complexity and simplicity.

12

Construction of Folds

Students often say, "I just can't draw folds," as if an inability to draw folds were an inherent defect. It probably just means these students haven't yet studied them. Once students take the time to understand folds, they find that drawing them can be a pleasure. Learning the common elements of fold construction— the way they're made—paves the way for you to draw any type of fold in any technique and drawings of any length. In this chapter, I'll also suggest some ways to draw folds.

Using Line and Tone to Draw Folds
In this drawing of a little Amish boy constructing his piglet barn, I used both line and tone to draw the folds. The folds on his shirt as it hangs over his pants show how hard he has been working.

UNDERSTANDING THE CONTOUR OF A FOLD

Liken each arrangement of folds to a miniature terrain with trails, hills, valleys, depressions and cliffs. The construction of the terrain doesn't change, but each time you change your view of the landscape, you see the construction in a different way. Similarly, every time you look at a fold from a different view, it appears different. Once you are able to understand and recognize the construction of a fold, you can use that knowledge to draw it from any angle.

1

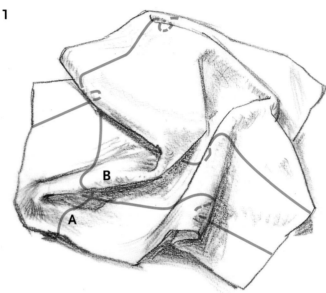

Different Views
Looking at the landscape of these folds from above (drawing 1), you can see the trail that begins at the bottom left edge of the fabric and climbs over hill A. You can follow that trail until it disappears under the fold of hill B. Imagine ants as they follow these trails over the folds. This helps you observe where the contour lines, or trails, disappear under folds and then reappear.

As you lower your view closer to eye level (drawing 2), the construction of the hills and valleys remains the same, but you see it differently. Beginning at the same spot, you can see only the contour line's ascent over hill A. The trail drops out of sight on the opposite side of the hill. Now, you can see the ascent rather than the descent on hill B.

2

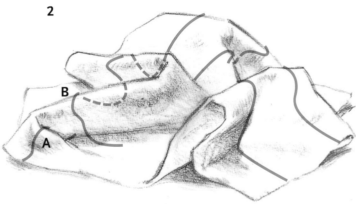

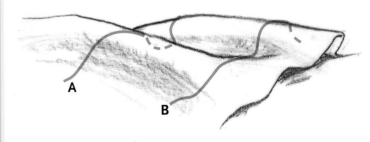

Overlaps and Changes of Plane
To understand folds, you must learn the difference between overlapping edges and changes of plane. Follow these two paths across different parts of the same fold. When path A reaches the crest, or edge of the hill, it disappears over the other side (indicated by a dotted line). You'd draw this part of the fold as an overlapping edge. Path B climbs over a more gently sloping part of the fold and back down the other side without passing out of view. The overlapping fold tapers into a change of plane at the spot where a cross-contour line remains in sight.

DRAWING OVERLAPPING EDGES & CHANGES OF PLANE

Knowing where and how to show overlapping edges or changes of plane will enable you to analyze and draw folds easily. Draw an overlapping edge with a hard stroke and a change of plane with a soft stroke. Remember this! These principles are the keys to drawing folds with authority. Hard means definite, and hard strokes are drawn crisply with a sharp medium. Soft suggests blurry, ragged or indefinite.

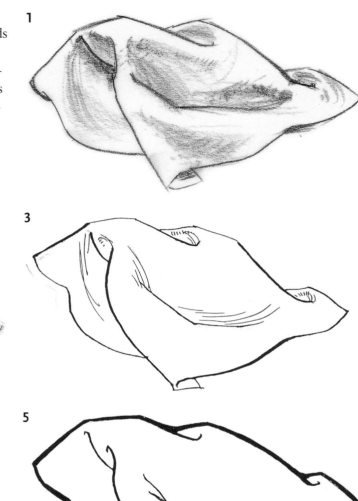

1

2

3

4

5

Applying Soft Strokes

You can see the hard, overlapping edges of these folds easily. Also notice some of the ways you can show soft changes of plane: the side of a sharp pencil (drawing 1), the side of a pastel stick (drawing 2), multiple pen strokes (drawing 3), a diluted wash of watercolor paint (drawing 4) and a hook at the end of a line (drawing 5).

FINDING FORMS IN FOLDS

quate each fold with one of the four basic geometric forms. Some folds resemble part of a cylinder or maybe a partial cone. Still others show changes of plane like those on cubes. Simple folds may closely resemble these simple geometric forms while others are more complex, their basic forms interrupted by bumps, dents and irregularities. Some folds begin like one geometric form and turn into another.

Basic Geometric Forms
Folds often follow the forms of a sphere, cone, cube or cylinder.

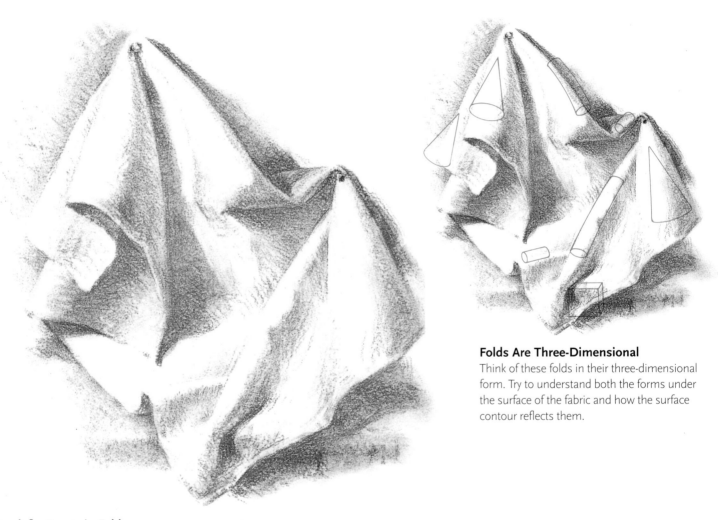

Folds Are Three-Dimensional
Think of these folds in their three-dimensional form. Try to understand both the forms under the surface of the fabric and how the surface contour reflects them.

Look for Forms in Folds
Three of the four basic geometric forms appear in the folds of this piece of fabric. Can you see them?

FINDING FORM WITH LIGHT AND SHADE

Once you identify the basic shape of the fold, apply the same principles of light and shadow to the folds as you would to basic shapes. Review the light and shadow terminology, applying it to folds as well as shapes:

- A highlight is the lightest part of the form, the part of the form closest to the light source.
- A cast shadow is the shadow that the form casts upon the surface upon which it sits.
- A core shadow is the darkest part of the form, the part that receives the least light.
- Reflected light is light that bounces back onto the form from the surface.
  Familiarize yourself with patterns of light and shadow. Experiment, using a bright lamp and objects similar to the four geometric shapes. Place each form on a surface made of a light value. Move the lamp around, observing changes in the location of light and shadow sides, cast shadows, core shadows, highlights and reflected lights. Observe places where value changes look like hard lines and where they are soft transitions.

Next, observe the objects when lit from the same direction but from varying distances. Note the variation of value intensity on the forms depending on how far away the light source is.

Once you're familiar with these common patterns of light and shadow, you can apply this knowledge to patterns on more complex forms in drapery.

highlight · core shadow · reflected light · cast shadow

Light Falling on a Sphere
As light falls on three-dimensional forms, you can usually see a light side, a shadow side and a cast shadow, but you can't always see the highlight, core shadow and reflected light. If the light source isn't very strong or the surface isn't very reflective or is light in value, the highlight may not be apparent. The lighter the surface on which a shadow is cast, the more reflected light shines back on the form and the more apparent is the core shadow.

USING TECHNIQUE TO INDICATE FORM

Apply tone to your folds in a way that either reinforces forms or doesn't cancel them out. Make sure your tone reinforces the direction of form or doesn't imply any directions at all. The point is to make sure you don't use tone that works against you. These principles of modelling, or shading, apply to folds, but your finger provides a handy example to study.

When indicating tone on a form that changes direction, change the direction of your strokes. Lift your medium between strokes so you can change the direction easily. You can't change direction in the middle of a zigzag stroke.

Study the Forms on Your Finger
Draw an imaginary line down the length of your finger. This shows the directions of the forms of your fingers. Then draw lines around your finger between each joint. These show how cross-contour lines would go around the forms. I used neutral tone on this finger, showing form with value but not indicating a direction.

1

2

3

Indicating Direction and Enhancing Form
You can use pencil strokes to indicate direction along the length of the form (drawing 1), cross-contour lines around the form (drawing 2) or both (drawing 3). Lines that indicate the direction of each form of the finger also make changes of direction apparent. Cross-contour lines enhance the form of the finger.

4

5

Making a Core Shadow
One way to indicate a core shadow is to draw neutral tone with the side of a pencil and then add cross-contour strokes around the form.

Don't Let Tone Conflict With Form
The zigzag strokes in drawing 4 don't follow the form of the finger. They work against it. In drawing 5, though, the diagonal strokes are very light and fine, and I've applied them in one direction, without zigzagging back and forth. These diagonal strokes don't work against the finger's form.

USING LINE AND TONE

You can draw folds using cross-contour lines, overlapping edges and changes of plane. It also helps to identify forms within the folds. You can combine line and tone, using tone to add three-dimensionality and line to add clarity.

1

2

Supplementing Line With Tone

You can draw the hard-edged overlap of a fold with line (drawing 1). Then you can supplement its form by using tone to suggest the change of plane on the near side of the fold (drawing 2).

Drawing Folds That Wrap Around Edges

When you look into a fold that wraps around an outside edge, you see the inner part of the fold as it also begins to wrap around the side. When drawing the overlapping edge of the fold with line, be sure to stop the line before it reaches the outside edge. If applying tone, change the hard line of the overlap to tone and also stop the tone before you reach the outside edge. The width of the gap between the end of the overlap line and the outside edge of the sleeve indicates the thickness of the fold.

If You Close the Gap, You Lose the Fold

When drawing a line to indicate an overlapping edge of a fold, don't continue it to the outside edge of the form. Without a gap to indicate the thickness of the fold, the fold will be lost.

Suggesting a Light Source

You can add mood to a drawing by suggesting a light source. The core shadows and cast shadows this light source would create also can reinforce and make clearer a figure's form. You don't have to do a fully modelled drawing to suggest a light source; you can add just a few shadows.

A Hint for Drawing Overlapping Folds

It's easy to get lost when drawing areas with several overlapping folds. To avoid this, draw the overlapping lines of primary folds first, ending each with a hook where you can go back and indicate a change of plane with tone. Once you've indicated the primary folds within a group, you can add supplemental tone to establish the folds' constructions. You can return later to model and add details.

Adding a Light Source to a Line Drawing

After drawing important overlapping edges, suggest shadow in a few places. I suggested changes of plane with strokes that followed the direction of each fold's form. Then I added core shadows with shorter lines in the direction of lines that wrap around each fold.

Cast Shadows

Cast shadows enhance form by emphasizing the outside edges of the form. Cast shadows also reinforce the forms over which they are cast by following their contour. Notice how a cast shadow follows the forms of the stretch folds on his left pant leg.

DRAWING FOLD STUDIES

Drawn as preliminaries to paintings, many fold studies by artists like Leonardo da Vinci, Albrecht Dürer and John Singer Sargent are magnificent pieces of art in themselves.

You can learn a great deal by doing a fold study of your own. Take all the time you need to analyze forms within the folds, to understand the way in which they receive light and to design them to your satisfaction.

Setting Up Your Own Fold Study

Select a piece of unwrinkled white fabric, sufficiently flexible to arrange but with enough body to form simple folds. Arrange the fabric into a pleasing design that includes folds of different types. Light the arrangement with one, consistent light source. Place the light so the forms are clear; so you can see cast shadows, areas of reflected light and core shadows; and so you like the effect. The following hints also will help make your study successful:

- Understand what you're drawing so you can verbally describe every inch of your study to another artist. Talk to yourself as you model the forms, using light and shadow terminology.
- Be consistent with the pattern of light and shadow. Avoid the spotty effect of misplaced contrast.
- Remember that you're an artist, not a photographer. You don't have to record an image exactly as you see it. Feel free to change the proportions of folds to improve design.
- Make sure your medium is sharp so you can draw clean, sharp, crisp edges whenever you need to.

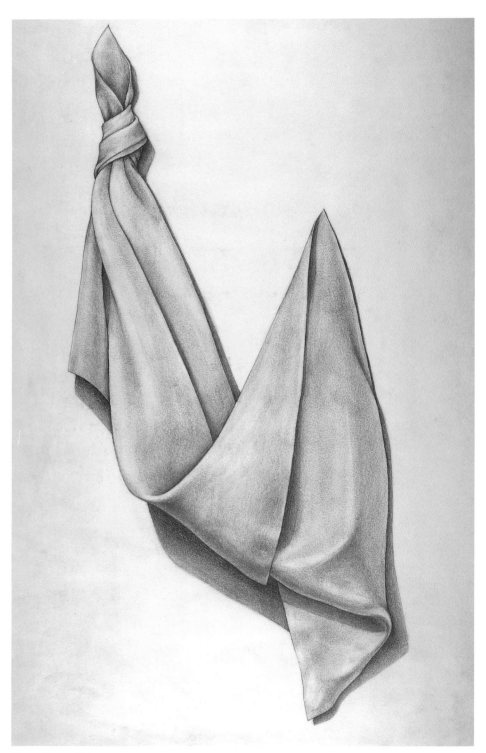

Form From Value
Student Sherrie Sinclair didn't use any visible pencil strokes for this study. She brought out the form of the folds solely with value.

Drawing Hints to Keep in Mind

- Think of the outside boundaries of your cloth as hard edges.
- Draw hard edges when the edge of a cast shadow falls evenly on a surface, but soften the edges of a cast shadow when it falls on a surface that is falling or turning away.
- Draw well-defined and sharp changes of plane with hard edges. Rounded changes of plane, such as those on a cylinder, are soft.
- Core shadows have soft edges.
- All objects are affected by atmospheric perspective. The farther away they are, the softer their edges appear. This usually isn't a factor when drawing figures and studies at a close distance, but you can diffuse edges to remove emphasis from one form, thereby emphasizing another.

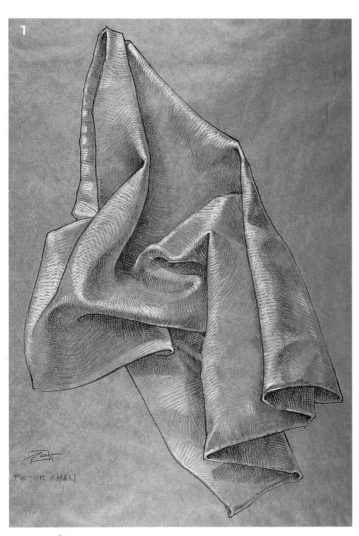

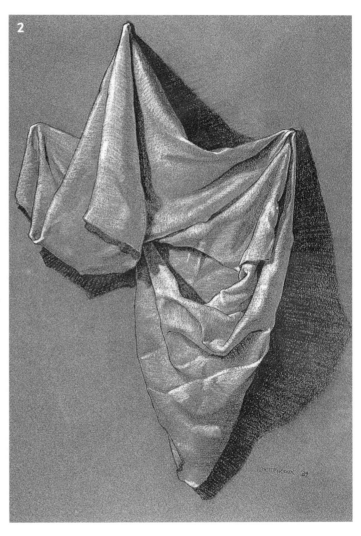

Try Toned Paper

After successfully modeling a fold study on white paper, try using toned paper and white pencil or chalk in addition to charcoal or pencil. This will teach you to pay as much attention to the light areas as the shaded areas. However, emphasizing light with white can be so exciting that it's easy to over-do it and become highlight-happy. Use white with restraint, reserving it for highlights on the light sides of forms where the light should be strongest and the light of the paper isn't sufficient. Also be careful not to let your white and toned media blend together.

Inspired Albrecht Dürer's woodcuts, Peter Chan carefully followed the forms of the folds with white and black pencils (drawing 1). Chris Bettencourt used charcoal and white pencils to indicate tone and light areas without visible strokes (drawing 2). This avoided a common danger: the direction of lines that indicate tone conflicting with the direction of the form .

JUST WHAT IS AN EDGE?

I've used the word "edge" several times in this chapter. Let's take a moment to see the many ways in which the term applies to figure drawing.

Edge of a Surface
It can be the edge of a drawing surface: a pad, canvas or piece of paper.

Edge of a Picture
An edge can be the outside boundaries of a picture within a drawing surface.

1

2

Edge of a Figure
It can be the outside edge of a figure, its entire outside shape.

Edge of a Shape
An edge can be the outside edges of shapes within a larger shape, such as the cuff of her sleeve, and overlapping forms within a shape, such as her arm laying across her lap.

Edge of an Object
An edge can mean the boundaries of a piece of fabric.

Edge of a Fold
An edge also can be the edge of an overlapping part within an object, such as the overlapping edge of a fold.

QUICK INDICATIONS OF FOLDS

When drawing unposed people or one- or two-minute poses, you don't have time to suggest more than the most useful folds. Still, these folds should reinforce the overall figure, design and gesture.

If you see some valuable folds of compression that affect an outside line, suggest them with a series of bumps on the outside line. Then use rapid strokes or tone to indicate the directions of the folds or the folds as they wrap around forms.

Don't worry about the construction of folds in these short sketches. Even in quick sketches, however, be sure to lift your medium from the surface with each stroke. This helps you control the direction of your strokes, curving them, fanning them out or gradually changing their directions.

Capture the Important Things
I liked this youth's slouching gesture, his haircut and his clothes. Compression folds appear along the front of his waist and along the inside of his arm. His baggy clothes also created wonderful compression folds on his sleeve and great stretch folds on his pants. These folds were a great help in communicating his slouch and baggy clothes.

Drawing a Dancer
This hip-hop dancer held this pose for about one minute. My priority was to capture the figure's design, but I also liked the way the stretch folds on his leg and the compression folds over his stomach brought out his gesture.

13

Types of Folds

Breaking down the types of folds into categories may seem removed from the purpose of drawing folds on people. But to be in control of the folds you draw, you have to know the characteristics of each type so you can recognize and use them to your advantage, blending them into a harmonious whole. In this chapter, you'll observe seven types of folds:

- pipe
- zigzag
- spiral
- half-lock
- diaper
- drop
- inert

Try to create and observe these folds yourself. You can arrange some with a piece of cloth. Others you can best observe by looking at your own clothing in a mirror. Look for patterns between similar gestures. Also observe that the same types of folds look different on different fabrics.

Look for Several Types of Folds
Five of the seven fold types—pipe, half-lock, diaper, drop and inert—appear in the abundant cloth of this Roman's toga. The more fabric there is, the more types of folds you'll see.

PIPE FOLDS

In their most regular pattern, pipe folds resemble a series of organ pipes, thus their name. Their shapes may be semicylindrical or semiconical. You see them everywhere from clothing to drapery. There are two varieties of pipe folds: relaxed and stretched.

1

2

Relaxed Pipe Folds

You see this type of pipe fold when fabric falls freely from a condensed area. Arrange a short end of a rectangle of cloth into pleats, grasping it at the top and letting the remaining fabric fall (drawing 1). These pipe folds, semicylindrical in shape and consistent in size, are the type you see in formal window draperies. To study irregular pipe folds (drawing 2), gather the material toward the top before letting the rest of the material fall. These pipe folds are semiconical in shape and vary more in size. Fabric gathered in waistbands show this kind of fold.

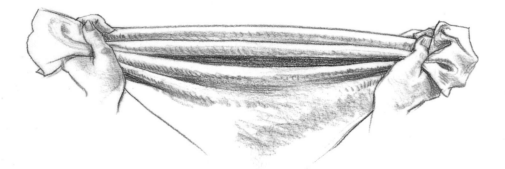

Stretched Pipe Folds

Fold a square of cloth into a triangle. Gather it near the upper corners and pull. This creates the cordlike pipe folds that appear in stretched fabric. You can also see these folds in rectangular fabric that has been gathered and pulled. However, diagonal fabric stretches more.

Zigzag Folds

igzag refers to the pattern of alternating folds that occurs on the inside of the bend of a tubular piece of fabric when the fabric buckles. To see zigzag folds, put on a jacket, put your hand in the pocket to bend your arm a bit and look in a mirror. When the tubular piece of cloth that makes up your sleeve bends, the stretching side of the cloth along the back of your arm becomes taut while the excess fabric on the inside buckles.

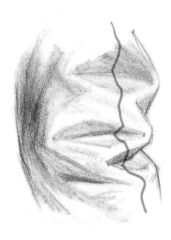

What Makes a Zigzag Fold?
Zigzag folds alternate directions. The nature of fabric affects the folds; the stiffer the fabric, the more angular the folds.

Planes of Zigzag Folds
Notice the horizontal diamond shapes. The top and bottom of each diamond fold toward each other to form two triangular planes meeting in the middle. Because the planes face different directions, each receives light differently.

Memory Zigzag Folds
This woman's knees are locked, not bent, but the cloth of her jeans has been bent so often that the folds have left an imprint. Study people waiting in line or standing on public transit. At the back of the knees of well-worn pants, you often see such zigzag folds caused by frequent compressions from bending the knees.

SPIRAL FOLDS

Spiral folds result when tubular pieces of cloth condense around tubular forms, such as a sleeve around an arm. Different gestures cause different directions of spiral folds, and variables like the amount and character of the fabric affect the number of folds that form. The more fabric condensed into one area, the more folds appear. The softer the fabric, the more typically rounded are the spirals.

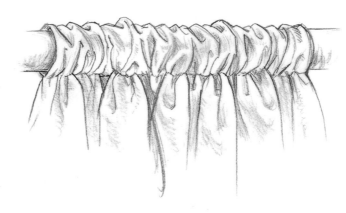

Spirals Form Around Cylinders
Cloth wrapped around curtain rods exhibits spiral folds. Notice the pipe folds that fall from the rod. Elastic in clothing, such as waistbands, creates similar but smaller spiral folds.

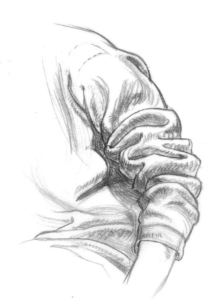

1   2

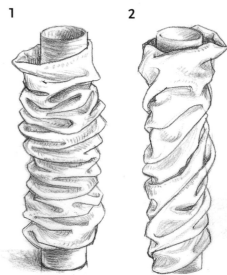

Condensed Fabric
Push the sleeve of a sweatshirt or soft sweater up your arm, condensing the fabric. Most of these folds actually form only partial spirals that don't go all the way around the form.

Direction Relates to Tension
The direction of spiral folds relates to the gesture of the underlying form. The tension between the armpit and elbow causes folds that travel diagonally between the two.

Create These Effects Yourself
You can make spiral folds by inserting a cardboard cylinder into a longer piece of fabric with the edges stapled together to form a cylinder. Soft cotton (drawing 1) makes typically rounded spiral folds. If you twist the fabric as you condense it (drawing 2), the folds spiral diagonally.

HALF-LOCK FOLDS

Half-lock folds occur when tubular pieces of cloth abruptly change direction. When a part of the figure abruptly changes direction, look for corresponding parts of the clothing that change direction. Then look for half-lock folds in these areas. Take advantage of half-lock folds to emphasize strong changes of direction.

Wrap Folds Around Outside Edges
Two half-lock folds appear at the bend of the inner arm in this drawing. Sometimes you'll see multiple half-lock folds, and sometimes you'll see a smaller half-lock inside a larger one. To make half-lock folds or any other fold look natural, pay attention to the way it wraps around the forms underneath. When drawing a fold as it wraps around a form, remember to continue the wraparound to the outer edge.

Half-Lock Folds From the Side
Half-lock folds are most obvious from the side. You can easily see them on sharply bent legs, arms and torsos.

Half-Lock Folds From the Front
The bulges of half-lock folds are visible on the sides of knees and elbows from a front view.

DIAPER FOLDS

D iaper folds form when fabric sags between two points of support. Folds form in directions that radiate from each point and meet between them. The low point of the sag where each fold meets the other may curve or bend sharply. The degree of the bend or curve depends on the amount of slack and the character of the fabric. The crisper a fabric is, the more angular is the break.

Classical, Byzantine and early medieval artists used diaper folds beautifully. Look for them particularly in cloaks, necklines and the slack areas between the knees of Madonnas, saints, angels and royalty.

Sagging Fabric
Hold a piece of fabric by its upper corners and allow the cloth to sag in the middle. When you hold your hands level, the dip will be centered between them.

Placing the Dip
When one point of support is higher than the other, the dip sits off-center, closer to the lower support.

Indicating Planes
Each fold has an upper and lower plane with a rounded transition between them. Also note that the more cloth that is gathered at the supporting points, the greater the number of folds that appear.

On the Bias
Diaper folds on a diagonal bias fall easily and are especially graceful. To observe diaper folds on the bias, fold your cloth into a triangle before making them.

On a Grecian Neckline
Diaper folds fall from this Grecian neckline, a style that has been used for thousands of years and still is seen today.

Drop Folds

The characteristic common to all drop folds is that fabric falls freely from a point or area of support. One simple fold or a complex unit of folds can fall from an area of support. Manipulating masses of drop folds gives you so many opportunities to bring life and vitality to your drawings and enhance their designs that I think of a drop fold as a gift to an artist.

Simple Drop Folds Are Conical
These simple drop folds that fall from a push pin are conical. You can bring out this conical quality by showing partial ellipses at the bottom edges of the folds.

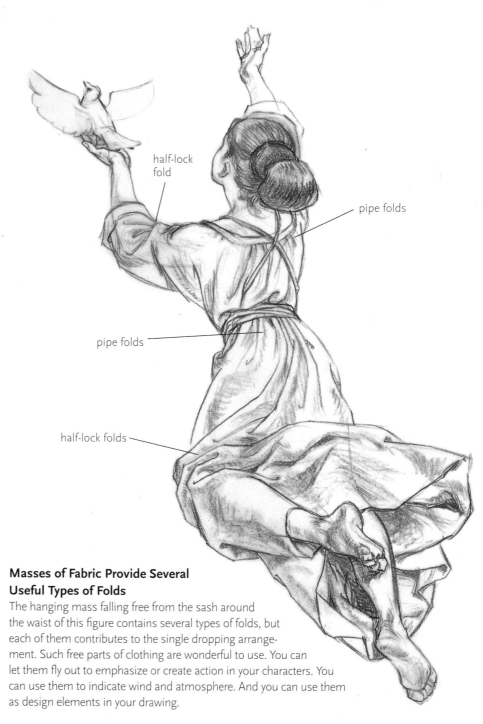

half-lock fold

pipe folds

pipe folds

half-lock folds

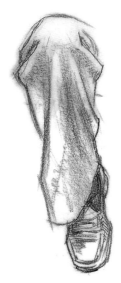

Drop Folds Fall From the Knee
You can almost always see a drop fold falling from the knee of a bent leg. Half-lock folds at the sides accompany the drop fold.

Masses of Fabric Provide Several Useful Types of Folds
The hanging mass falling free from the sash around the waist of this figure contains several types of folds, but each of them contributes to the single dropping arrangement. Such free parts of clothing are wonderful to use. You can let them fly out to emphasize or create action in your characters. You can use them to indicate wind and atmosphere. And you can use them as design elements in your drawing.

INERT FOLDS

I nert folds are sometimes called "dead folds," but they can add so much beauty to a drawing that "inactive" is a more appropriate term. As with drop folds, a mass of inert folds may contain several other types of folds, but the entire mass itself is considered inert.

Though the mass of folds is inert, you can suggest any movement just finished. In your drawings, you can arrange extra fabric of long garments into inert folds to suggest any action a character has just taken or the direction from which a figure has come.

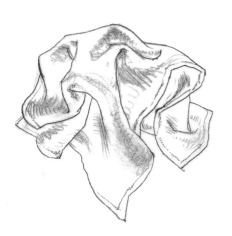 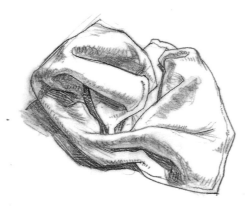 

Folds Within an Inert Mass Can Change

Drop some cloth on the floor, crumpling it first to make sure it shows some form. Then pick it up and drop it again. The folds within the mass change each time, but the mass itself remains inert, not indicating any movement.

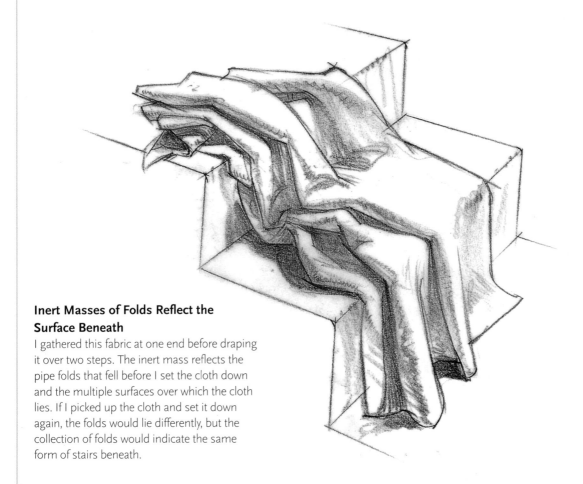

Inert Masses of Folds Reflect the Surface Beneath

I gathered this fabric at one end before draping it over two steps. The inert mass reflects the pipe folds that fell before I set the cloth down and the multiple surfaces over which the cloth lies. If I picked up the cloth and set it down again, the folds would lie differently, but the collection of folds would indicate the same form of stairs beneath.

14

Drawing Folds on People

The folds you draw on clothing can really bring your people to life. Having learned about types and construction of folds, you now can put them to work to express your opinions about the people and actions you're drawing. You can control folds to tell the story you want to tell.

Enhance Your Drawings With Folds
Remain aware of the body's continuity under the clothing. Then you can have fun drawing details that add to the story you're telling and enhance design. You can manipulate loose areas of fabric any way you like. I made this cavalier's sleeves and breeches fuller and contrasted those elements with tighter cuffs. I made his boots wider and added the spurs and collar, details from the seventeenth century. I used folds on these elements to intensify his gesture.

FINDING THE BODY UNDER CLOTHING

To draw people in clothing, you must be aware of the figure beneath the clothing. Finding the figure is easy when clothes fit closely. Under full clothing, look for clues that reveal the location of parts of the body essential to the gesture. The cavalier on this page is debonair, confident and a trifle arrogant. I used drawing aides to find his form beneath his clothing, then used the interesting characteristics of his seventeenth-century garments to help tell a story.

Find Relationships and Rhythms
These relationships and rhythms communicate a relaxed, confident attitude. His torso's rhythm also establishes the center of his back, which I needed to place the center of his collar.

Look for Clues
Look for areas where clothing lies directly over the body. This helps you locate the figure's forms. You also can mentally connect outside edges to establish continuity.

Find Wraparounds
Parts of clothing that wrap around the body increase solidity and help indicate the directions of parts of the body.

Look for Folds That Enhance a Gesture
These folds help indicate the cavalier's arrogant gesture. You can manipulate flowing, loose areas of clothing to enhance design and communicate what you want about a person. On this drawing, these free areas were the loose cloth on his sleeves and pant legs and the cuffs on his boots.

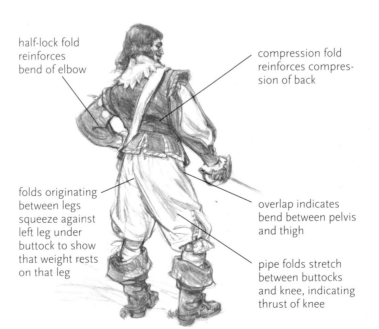

half-lock fold reinforces bend of elbow

compression fold reinforces compression of back

folds originating between legs squeeze against left leg under buttock to show that weight rests on that leg

overlap indicates bend between pelvis and thigh

pipe folds stretch between buttocks and knee, indicating thrust of knee

FINDING THE TORSO

The shirts on these figures have full bodies and sleeves, which makes finding the forms of the figure just a bit more difficult. Look for areas where clothing lies directly over the form of the body, such as shoulders, wrists, elbows and sashes, to help establish lines of continuity.

shoulders, sash and cuffs indicate figure's form

pants show thrusting hip

compression folds show form of thigh

areas between folds follow form of leg

Drawing Aides Help Him Lean Away

This cavalier's right hip is higher than his left hip, and his back and far side stretch as he leans and twists. His sash overlaps his shirt to indicate his form, except for some surplus fabric from his shirt that overlaps his sash to reinforce the compression of his right side. Even though the top edge of his sash is covered, the bottom edge can still tell you that his right hip is higher than his left.

Drawing Aides Help Him Lean Forward

This cavalier's shirt overlaps the top edge of his sash, and the bottom of his sash overlaps his pants. These two overlapping forms work together to indicate a general forward direction. I had fun indicating his quick twisting motion with his hair and flying sash. Note the stretch and compression folds on his shirt that indicate the twisting and leaning motion.

In Perspective

Your view of this buccaneer is so far below eye level that the outside edges of his shirt disappear behind his sash and pants. These corners are important in communicating extreme perspective. Again, the areas where clothes lie immediately over the forms of his body help locate the torso. His pigtails and the pipe folds of his shirt follow the direction of his back. Pipe folds from the back of his waist wrap around his left buttock before stretching out toward his knee. Pipe folds that start at the front of his pants travel between his legs and stretch toward the back of his right leg. These two groups of pipe folds combine to emphasize the thrust from the back of his right leg to his left knee.

DRAWING FOLDS OVER LEGS

Students often forget that visible parts of legs and ankles are attached to legs beneath pants, skirts or gowns. Then the students draw the visible parts of the legs as if they were stuck to the bottom edge of the clothing.

To draw clothing over concealed legs, look for clues to the locations, actions and rhythms of the legs. Then draw whatever you can see of the legs or ankles before drawing the garments. This lets you wrap hems around the forms of the legs, keep the legs in proportion, make adjustments to the length of the garments and avoid bad tangents.

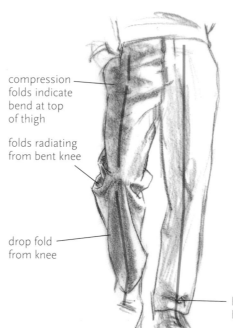

compression folds indicate bend at top of thigh

folds radiating from bent knee

drop fold from knee

half-lock fold indicates bend at ankle

Drawing Folds on Upright Legs
The subtle rhythms through this figure's leg make the gesture look natural. Before drawing pants over upright legs, determine the action and resulting rhythm of each leg and locate each foot in relation to the hips. Next, draw each foot. Then you can go back to draw the outside edges of the pants, any hems that wrap around the feet and the folds you need to enhance the gesture or character of clothing.

1

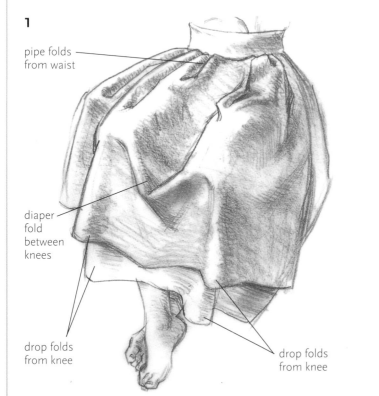

pipe folds from waist

diaper fold between knees

drop folds from knee

drop folds from knee

2

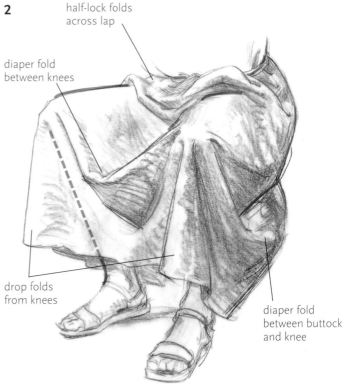

half-lock folds across lap

diaper fold between knees

drop folds from knees

diaper fold between buttock and knee

Drawing Folds on Seated Figures
In seated figures, locate the waist, buttocks, lap where the legs leave the pelvis, knees and feet. Before drawing any folds, draw any parts of the garments that lie immediately over the body. In drawing 1, the woman's knees and left thigh are apparent through her skirt. You can establish continuity by drawing imaginary lines between these points and any exposed forms, such as this woman's feet and ankles. After I located the forms of her legs and drew her ankles and feet, the folds were easy and fun to draw. The diaper fold and drop folds on drawing 2 show the location of his knees, and the gathered material over his thighs indicate his lap.

DRAWING GROUPS OF FOLDS

When clothing is made of voluminous fabric, you can categorize folds into groups. Each group has a source area (the place from which it begins) and one or more destinations. The destination of a group may be a specific place or places or an area where the group dissipates or turns into another group.

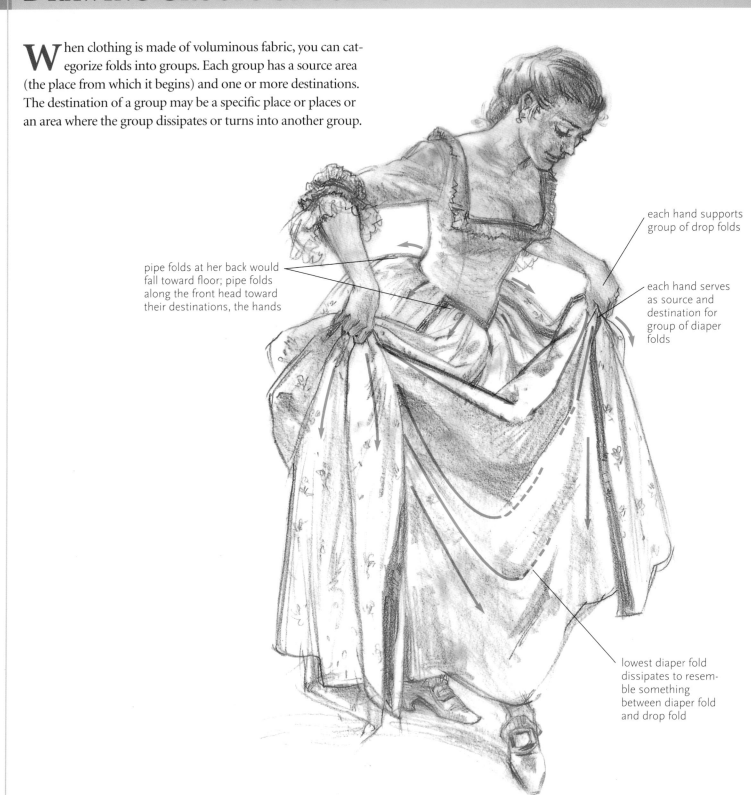

each hand supports group of drop folds

each hand serves as source and destination for group of diaper folds

pipe folds at her back would fall toward floor; pipe folds along the front head toward their destinations, the hands

lowest diaper fold dissipates to resemble something between diaper fold and drop fold

Analyzing Groups of Folds

Before drawing this woman's skirt, I had to locate her legs and feet and understand their rhythms. Then I drew the visible parts of her feet and finally her skirt. This procedure allowed me to draw her skirt whatever way I wanted, whether longer or fuller or shorter or less full.

LOOKING FOR CLUES

Finding the form of the body under voluminous clothing is difficult because there are few visible clues to help you locate the figure's forms. First determine the attitude and emotions of the figure you want to convey. Then look for clues, such as the location of feet and areas of clothing that lie immediately over the body.

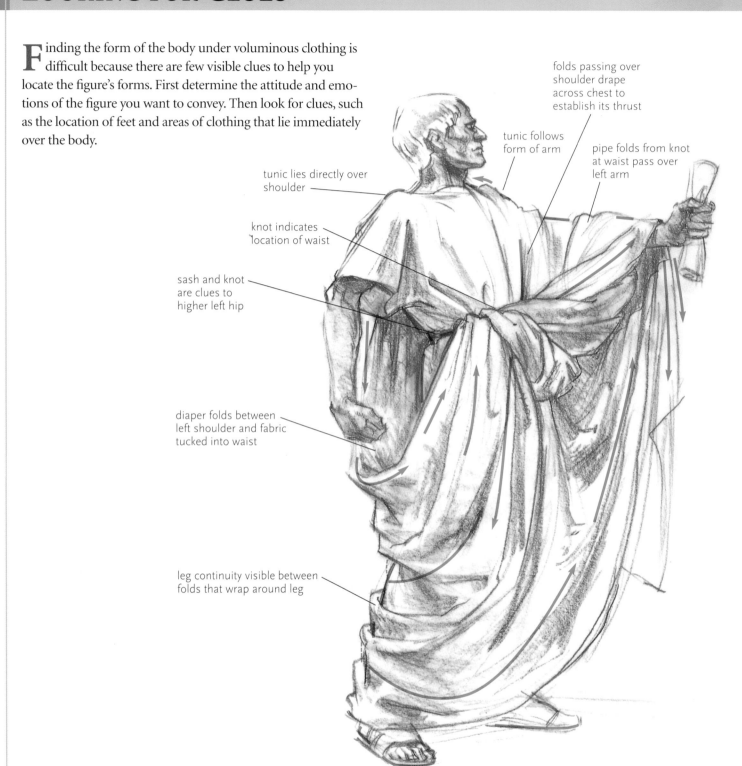

folds passing over shoulder drape across chest to establish its thrust

tunic follows form of arm

pipe folds from knot at waist pass over left arm

tunic lies directly over shoulder

knot indicates location of waist

sash and knot are clues to higher left hip

diaper folds between left shoulder and fabric tucked into waist

leg continuity visible between folds that wrap around leg

Analyzing Attitude and Emotion

The rhythm of this figure is one long curve. Notice areas where clothing lies immediately over his body. These clues help establish his authoritative stance. Study the folds that follow and cross over his forms. Some of the folds that pass over his left shoulder go diagonally across his back and around his right leg. Many of these begin as pipe folds from his shoulder and turn into diaper folds as they travel around his leg. If I had wanted to show action, I would have drawn the folds over his arm flying out.

5 DRAWING CLOTHING

As you draw from life, translating reality

to your version of it on paper, changes inevitably will occur. Our challenge as

artists is to make each change a positive one—a change that works for a

drawing, not against it. If your goal is an accurate representation of the sub-

ject, your changes may be minor, merely to improve design or the fit of a gar-

ment. Or, if you want to tell a story with your drawing, you may want to

change more, altering the clothing's style, fit and details. The next two chap-

ters will introduce you to the way clothing is made and give you hints for

drawing it. The purpose of these chapters is to give you greater control of the

people you draw wearing the clothes you want them to wear.

15

Elements of Clothing

To draw clothing convincingly, you need not be a tailor, but knowing a little about the way clothes are made helps you interpret what you see and enables you to control how clothing looks on your people. This chapter discusses factors that affect how garments look on the people who wear them.

Choose Clothing That Suits Your Story
Fabric on the bias is flexible, so clothing cut on the bias tends to cling to the body. Slim, glamorous evening gowns like this one from the 1930s were cut on the bias to reveal the curves of the figure.

Direction and Weave

Extremely important to the way clothing looks on a person is the direction of a piece of fabric's weave as it drapes on a figure: Is the pattern cut on the straight or on the bias? Fabric that is cut along its length or width as it was manufactured is cut on the straight. Fabric cut on the bias is cut diagonally.

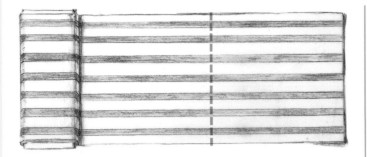

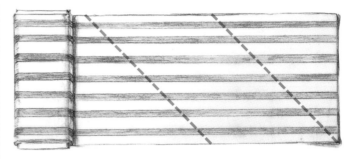

Fabric Cut on the Straight

Fabric cut parallel to its length or width is cut on the straight and has little or no give. This skirt was made from fabric cut on the straight and gathered along its length. To make a vertically striped skirt the manufacturers would have gathered it along the width.

Fabric Cut on the Bias

Fabric cut diagonally is cut on the bias and stretches. Manufacturers would have made this diagonally striped skirt from four pieces of the same fabric cut on the bias.

Gathered Fabric

Some of the earliest depictions of clothing show garments of fabric compressed around the waist. Gathering fabric into a smaller area still is a common form of clothing construction. You'll see fabric gathered at the waistbands of full skirts and at the wrists of full sleeves. You also can compress clothing yourself with sashes, belts, even the belt around your bathrobe.

Sources of compression release gathered folds. When you draw these irregular pipe folds, make sure they begin at the source. On a skirt, some folds will be short, some will continue to the hem along the bottom of the skirt, and some will diffuse somewhere in between.

A Collar Cut on the Bias
The folds on this collar, which is made of fabric cut on the bias, are convex and fall outward and downward.

Gathered on the Straight
When material is gathered on the straight, such as the horizontally striped skirt on page 123, the folds that result are convex, curving outward. The fuller and crisper the fabric, the greater the curve.

Gathered on the Bias
When material is gathered on the bias, such as the diagonally striped skirt on page 123, the folds that fall are concave. This "caving in" of folds is characteristic of fabric cut on the bias. Only near the source, where the material is gathered, are the folds convex.

Cut on the Bias But Not Gathered
This skirt, cut along the bias, wasn't gathered at all. The waistband and the material used to make it measure the same, so the folds begin at the hips where the fabric becomes fuller than the form beneath.

Drawing Hems

Folds that travel all the way down to the hem affect the way the edges of the hem appear. To show their semiconical form, draw these edges as partial ellipses.

Edges of Folds Follow Forms of Folds

The clothing of this Navajo girl shows three sources of compression where fabric has been gathered: (1) her belt compresses her blouse, so I drew the edges of the blouse with slight ellipses, (2) the skirt is gathered at the hidden waistband; to show the forms of any pipe folds that travel from the waistband to the ribbon running around her skirt, I drew the ribbon with partial ellipses, and (3) more folds fall from the ribbon two-thirds of the way down her skirt. I drew the edges of the folds on the ruffle with partial ellipses to indicate the conical shapes of the folds.

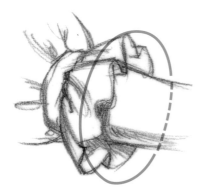
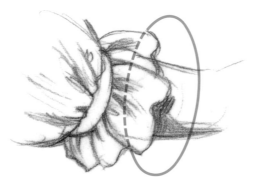

Draw Elliptical Edges

To make your figures and their parts look more three dimensional, do not draw the edges of fabric with straight lines. Draw fabric from a view in which the edges look like ellipses. The depth of the ellipse depends on how extreme the view is. When the form is coming toward you, draw the edges as if you're looking into or under the edge of the fabric. When the form is heading away from you, draw the edges as if you're looking down over them.

PLEATED FABRIC

Cloth can be compressed in a more orderly fashion by pleating. Just as you do when drawing gathered material, pay attention to how the pleated folds descend from their source and how the folds affect the edges.

Unpressed Pleats

This dancer gathered her sari to form irregular pleats and tucked them. They fall gracefully from the elastic waist. Her extended foot opens some pleats, but others flow from the waist all the way to the hem. The zigzag edges are rounded as opposed to the angular zigzags on the pressed pleats of the kilt.

Pressed Pleats

The pressed pleats of a kilt begin at the waist and are stitched as far as the line of the hip. Draw the edges of pleats with sharp zigzag lines, opening some more than others to indicate movement.

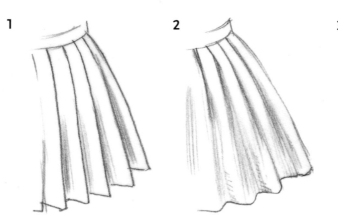

Study How the Pleats Hang

Pressed pleats (drawing 1) hang differently than unpressed pleats (drawing 2). Whether they overlap (drawings 1 and 2) or fan out like an accordion (drawing 3) also affects how they hang.

THICKNESS

Indicate the thickness of fabric with the edges of garments, the edges of overlapping parts of clothing and the overlapping edges of folds. These places may be small, but they're extremely useful in establishing the character of the clothing.

1

2

Compare Thickness of Fabrics
The jacket and sweater in drawing 1 are made of thin wool, and those in drawing 2 are made of thicker wool. Notice the difference in thickness where the sweater wraps around the neck, where the lapel wraps around the neck, where the lapel wraps around the shoulder, at the corner of the lapel, where the two sections of the lapel meet and on the right lapel near the button.

1

2

Use Double Lines and Corners
In both of these drawings, the protrusion of the belt from the side of the waist indicates the thickness of the belt. In drawing 1, I also showed thickness by drawing a double line wherever the viewer could see the thickness of the belt or buckle. In drawing 2, I used double lines on the laces and eyelets.

TEXTURE

Use edges. Whether you choose to suggest texture by fully modeling it, combining line and tone or using just line, always show texture at the outside edges of the garment.

Indicating Form and Texture With Line

I used line to show the texture of ribbing on the upper and lower edges of this rolled collar and to show the cable knit of the sweater on the outside edge of his shoulder. I also indicated the surface texture of the ribbing and knit. When drawing texture like this, make sure the lines follow the form of the body. The ribs of the collar as viewed in perspective brought out the form of the collar as it wrapped around his neck. At the upper corners of the collar, you can see ribs wrapping into the inside of the collar.

Reinforcing Form and Texture With Tone

I added tone to the line for this drawing, bringing out the curve of the collar with a shadow. I also added a little shadow to the cable knit pattern to make it look more three-dimensional.

1   **2**   **3**

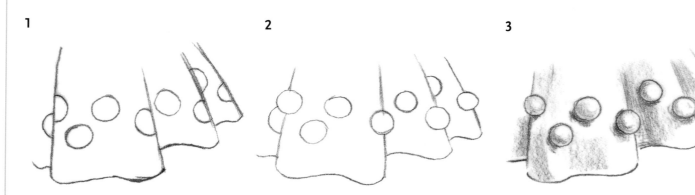

Printed Pattern or Three-Dimensional Texture?

The circles on the folds in drawing 1 look like printed polka dots. By adjusting just four of the circles so they overlap edges, I've made the skirt look like it has pompoms attached instead (drawing 2). I enhanced the three-dimensional appearance by adding shading to the folds and adding cast shadows and core shadows to the pompoms (drawing 3).

Quilting

The thick, padded quilting affects the outside edges and surface texture of the cuff. I drew the diamond shapes in perspective and added tone to their shadows to bring out their forms.

Shearling

You don't have to show shadow texture over the entire surface of shearling. I indicated texture on the outside edges and then added tone to only part of the shadow side.

Fur

I indicated texture on the outside edges of this cuff by drawing hairs in the direction in which they grew or in the direction they wrapped around the edge. Drawing just a few hairs on the shadow side was enough to indicate the fur texture of the entire cuff.

16

Tips for Drawing Clothing

Headgear, footwear and clothing can enhance character and reinforce three-dimensionality. But artists sometimes miss the mark. They might draw clothes meant to look new actually appearing slept in; symmetrical garments might look lopsided; the forms beneath the garments might look distorted or flat.

Once you know how to draw clothing that fits well, you can make any changes you want, changing clothes that don't fit well to garments that look tailored and vice versa. You can even change contemporary clothing to period clothing. The tips in this chapter will help you see better, use what you see, change what you see or even develop a person from your mind.

You Can Change Your Figure
This model posed in a corset and undergarments from 1900, but her shoes were contemporary with small heels. I changed her shoes to boots and altered her hair style to help her fit the time period.

DRAWING NECKLINES AND COLLARS

To draw a neckline or collar convincingly, you need to understand its intended style, condition and fit, the perspective, the wearer's attitude and, most importantly, the forms beneath.

Wraparounds and perspective can work together to benefit your drawings. Don't let them cancel each other out. Use any wraparound and be aware of how perspective affects this wraparound. Whenever you draw a curve that shows a collar's style, also make sure you show the form of the body beneath it.

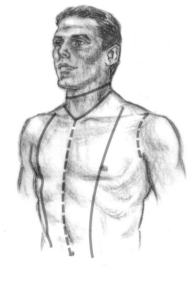

Visualize the Form Under Clothing

For clues to drawing necklines, visualize lines that wrap around a figure's neck, each trapezius and the shoulders. Imagine lines that run down the centers of the front and back and use them to place buttons, zippers and other details. Always be aware of the location of the body's natural waistline and shoulders. Then you can compare and draw a garment with a high or low waistline or a sleeve that begins off the shoulder convincingly.

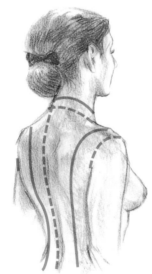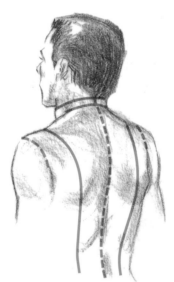

MODIFYING COLLAR STYLES

Once you understand how to draw close-fitting collars, you can modify them in style and character by making small adjustments or completely changing the type of collar. Here's a hint: To lend smartness to a lapel, slightly flatten some of the curves ; in contrast, excessive curves make garments look unkempt.

Collars Reflect Form
The collar reflects the neck's form, and the lapel reflects the form of the trapezius. Make the lapel and corresponding points on collars symmetrical (in perspective). Draw the buttons on a single-breasted suit along the figure's center line.

Keep Continuity in Mind
When a head thrusts forward, a gap often appears between the back of the neck and the collar. Keep the continuity between the shoulders beneath the collar and the neck in mind.

Use the Centerline
I located the centerline of this figure and then changed his collar and lapels to make his coat look like one from 1810. Each point on his lapel and each row of buttons is equidistant from the centerline (in perspective). Locating the centerline also will help you draw necklines and collars on various gestures, such as a slouching figure.

Fitted and Relaxed Collars
Form is less noticeable beneath relaxed collars and garments, but it is there. I used the seams of his pockets to suggest the form of the chest.

You Can Adjust Standing Collars
You can do anything you want with standing collars as long as you are aware of the head, neck and shoulders beneath them.

MODIFYING SHAPES

The word "shape" as applied to garments can refer to two things: the intrinsic shape of an article of clothing or the shape when viewed in perspective. Keep the garment's intrinsic shape in mind, but modify it to better communicate your viewpoint if the shape works against perspective. You can alter the shape slightly so it appears unchanged but no longer works against your viewpoint.

1

2

3

Modify the Shape to Communicate Your View

The intrinsic shape of a corset, as viewed from the front at eye level, appears in drawing 1. When the figure wearing the corset leaned toward me (drawing 2), I made the upward curve at the center of the top edge less pronounced and emphasized the curves around the lower edge. When the figure leaned away from me (drawing 3), I drew the opposite, emphasizing the upward curves and downplaying the downward curves.

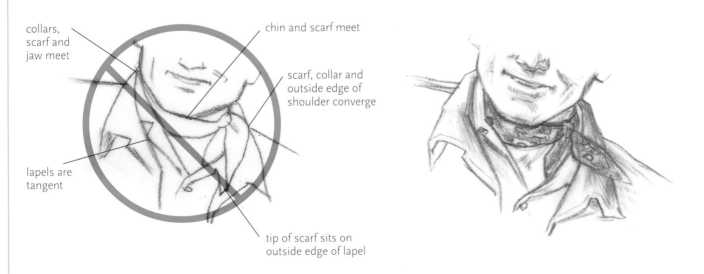

collars, scarf and jaw meet

chin and scarf meet

scarf, collar and outside edge of shoulder converge

lapels are tangent

tip of scarf sits on outside edge of lapel

Avoid Tangents!

Don't accept misleading tangents—places at which one overlapping form appears tangent to another, meaning they seem to just touch rather than overlap. Offset the forms to create depth. Even if your model's clothes have tangents in reality, make adjustments to suggest that the elements are different depths.

INDICATING BODY TYPE

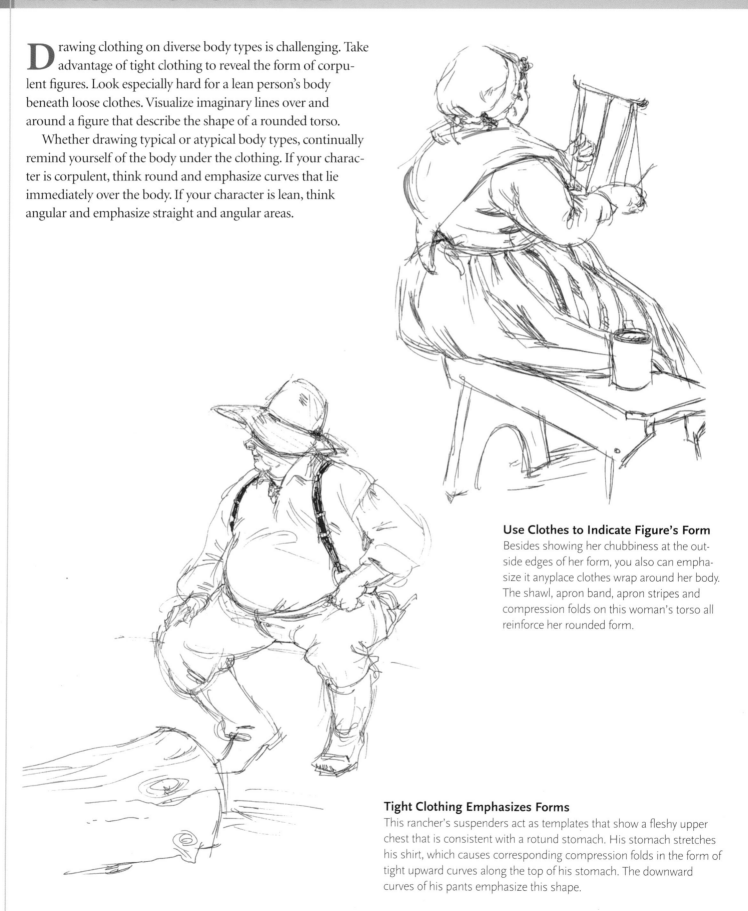

Drawing clothing on diverse body types is challenging. Take advantage of tight clothing to reveal the form of corpulent figures. Look especially hard for a lean person's body beneath loose clothes. Visualize imaginary lines over and around a figure that describe the shape of a rounded torso.

Whether drawing typical or atypical body types, continually remind yourself of the body under the clothing. If your character is corpulent, think round and emphasize curves that lie immediately over the body. If your character is lean, think angular and emphasize straight and angular areas.

Use Clothes to Indicate Figure's Form
Besides showing her chubbiness at the outside edges of her form, you also can emphasize it anyplace clothes wrap around her body. The shawl, apron band, apron stripes and compression folds on this woman's torso all reinforce her rounded form.

Tight Clothing Emphasizes Forms
This rancher's suspenders act as templates that show a fleshy upper chest that is consistent with a rotund stomach. His stomach stretches his shirt, which causes corresponding compression folds in the form of tight upward curves along the top of his stomach. The downward curves of his pants emphasize this shape.

Loose Clothing on Lean Figure

To show clothing that is too big for a person, pay special attention to the continuity and rhythm of the body. Look for visible clues to essential parts of the body. Once you've found the body's form, you can emphasize the looseness of the clothes. The narrowness of this youth's hip and the shirt's vertical drop reinforce the fact that there is a slight body under baggy clothing.

Use Knees and Elbows to Indicate Build

Imagine a patch on pants at the knee of a bent leg. The patch represents the part of the fabric that lies directly above the form of the knee, and folds emanate from this area of tension. The size of the patch should match the figure's build. The plumper the knee, the larger the patch. This principle also applies to elbows.

DRAWING HATS AND HOODS

When drawing any type of head covering, as always, be aware of the form beneath, even if the hat is made of stiff material. Once you learn to draw a hat to fit a head, you easily can figure out how to draw an infinite variety of headgear, including hats that don't necessarily fit the head.

Draw Hats to Fit Heads

Hats usually have crowns—the part that sits on your head—and brims that flare out from the head. Both provide character, but the crown is the place to draw hats that fit. Liken the base of the crown to a narrow band that wraps around the head. Locate the placement of that band, temporarily ignoring the brim, then draw the crown upward. Finish by drawing the brim, using it to add style and design that work in your composition.

Perspective and Design

Perspective affects the way you see crowns and brims. Before drawing the shapes of the crown and brim, look for straighter parts of the curves. They'll help you see the curves accurately and avoid a mechanical look. They also can improve the design of your drawing.

Hats Can Convey Attitude

Once you learn to draw a hat that looks natural and fits the head, experiment with how the person wears the hat. These men wear the same hat differently. I drew facial expressions that reflect the attitude suggested by the angle of each hat.

Drawing Large Brims

Large brims on bonnets have interesting shapes of their own. Still, being aware of the head is as important when drawing a bonnet as when drawing any other hat. You still need to understand exactly where the crown rests and the brim begins its own form. Imagine the curve of the forehead and the place where the crown rests on the head in drawing 1. If you tip the head, match that tilt with the symmetrical parts of the hat, as in drawing 2.

1

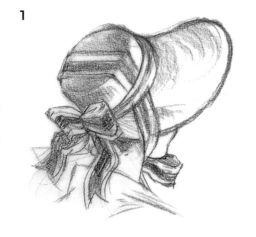

2

Hats That Stand Away From the Head

The crowns on some hats stand away from the head, and the supports underneath the crown conform to the head.

Hoods

When drawing people wearing hoods, be especially conscious of what is under the hood. Locate the shoulders as well the head. Decide which parts of the hood will rest on the head and which parts will lie on the shoulders. Then you can alter the rest of the hood as you wish to suit the gesture and design.

DRAWING FOOTWEAR

There are two different approaches to drawing shoes. One is to see the shapes. The other is to analyze what is happening. Looking at the shapes helps you learn about the odd shapes that occur when you view shoes in perspective. Seeing the shape also helps you accept the peculiar characteristics of different types of footwear. Analyzing helps you understand what you see so you can draw it as it truly is, alter it or develop shoes in your head.

The ideal method is to combine these approaches, accepting the shapes that are there and analyzing them to convey what you want.

Copying the Shape

Copying the outside shapes of shoes exactly, whether from life or photos, shows you the intrinsic shapes of different styles of shoes and the variations of these shapes when seen in perspective.

Analyzing

First consider the foot inside the shoe. Is it a right or left foot? Are you viewing the inner or outer side? What direction is it facing? What are the foot and ankle doing? Then consider the shoe. Is the heel higher than the sole? Does perspective affect what you see? Which parts of the shoe wrap around the foot, reinforcing the foot's form and general direction? Note that the soles of these shoes, like most flat shoes, bend upward slightly at the toe.

convex

concave

concave

convex

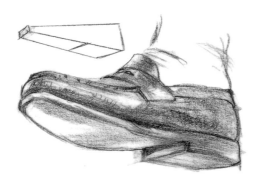

Look for the Simple Shape

To quickly analyze the direction and perspective of a shoe that has little or no heel, visualize it as a truncated wedge. Then you can add the extra shape and variation of that shape particular to a certain style. When a shoe is off the ground, as when the wearer is walking, visualize the wedge in space. When a shoe bends, visualize the wedge bending.

Envision the Foot First

To draw a woman's dress shoe, draw the foot first, lifting the heel according to the height of the shoe heel and establishing rhythm from the ankle through the foot. The height of the heel affects the rhythm through the ankle and foot. The higher the heel, the more likely you'll see a compound curve.

To show the foot's direction, visualize a line drawn from the shoe heel base through the base of the ball of the foot, as in these dotted lines. Then build the shoe around the foot, adding the sole and heel and any straps that wrap around the foot.

Look for Change of Direction in Ankle

When drawing shoes from the front, you may not notice the diagonal relationship between the ankle bones or the foot's change of direction at the ankle, but you must look for them. If you draw the form of the foot and shoe correctly but miss such things, the attitude of the foot will not look natural.

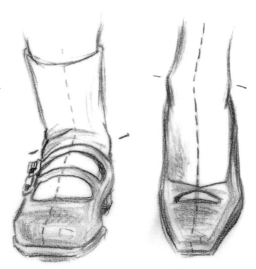

DRAWING OTHER KINDS OF FOOTWEAR

Some types of footwear are more difficult to draw than others. The bulk and complexity of athletic shoes present a challenge, and loose areas of boots make it easy to lose the continuity of the legs and feet inside them.

  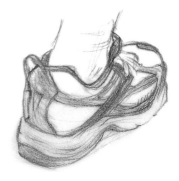

Athletic Shoes

Use the same principles you used when drawing other shoes, locating the form of the foot first. Add the tongue and heel, the irregular shape of the sole and decorative detail afterwards to create interest and, as always, to show form and direction.

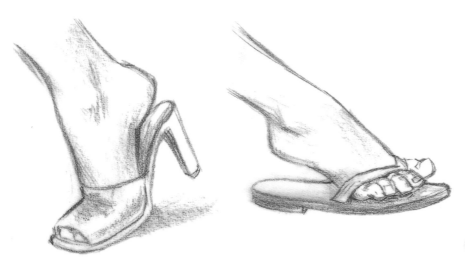 

Drawing Shoes That Don't Follow the Form of the Foot

Take advantage of the interesting things that occur when a shoe doesn't entirely correspond with the foot, such as the action when the heel leaves a backless shoe while the wearer is walking or a child's foot in her mother's shoe. These occurrences provide opportunities to tell stories.

1

2

3

Continuity Plus Character

Look for the continuity of a leg within a boot. Notice boot areas that do correspond with the leg and foot and those that don't. Look for patterns in the style of the boot. Rubber boots (drawing 1) have loose legs so the wearer can put them on easily. They also have treaded soles and a bulge at the back of the heel. Western boots (drawing 2) fit close around the feet and looser around ankles and calves. They have tapered toes and high heels that slant inward. Riding boots (drawing 3) are close-fitting around the calves. They're made of softer leather than western boots, so you can often see folds at the looser ankle area.

1

2

Use Loose Areas to Enhance Gesture

Compression folds form on the soft, loose leather of this seventeenth-century cavalier's boots, corresponding with the stretch and compression of his ankles. These actions enhance the actions of his feet, legs and entire figure. The leg in drawing 1 is leaning forward and the leg in drawing 2 is leaning back.

6

DRAWING EXTRAS

FROM WHAT YOU'VE LEARNED AND OBSERVED IN

this book, you now can bring greater life and fluidity and a more natural feel

to all the people you draw. The following chapters address subjects that will

give your drawings of people and children that final authority. You'll learn

about designing figures and how you can use that design to help tell the story

you want to tell. You'll learn about drawing facial expressions, hands and eld-

erly people. The last chapter discusses the most difficult subject of all: chil-

dren. You then can put all of these things together to draw any person you

want, young or old, doing what you want him or her to do. You truly can

make your drawings your own.

17

Design of the Figure

Design Elements in Clothing
You don't always have to draw a figure as it is.
You can emphasize or adjust parts of clothing
to facilitate the design of your drawing. In this
figure, curved lines contrast straight ones and
simple areas contrast complex ones.

Not everyone who views a picture is conscious of
design, but everyone responds to good design.
Whether powerful, exciting or pleasing, it adds immea-
surably to the effectiveness of any piece of art.

Good design enhances a story while strengthen-
ing the scene's composition. The relationship between
figures makes a design. A single figure can constitute a
design. Even the arrangement of folds on a figure's
clothing creates a design. All other skills being equal,
an artist's awareness of design can be the single element that makes his or her work superior.

Many students, particularly those who love to
draw detail in figure drawing, groan inwardly with impa-
tience when they hear the word "design". I confess that
I was one of them once. But somehow, whether
through observing the work of artists I admire or
through experience, the element of design became
increasingly fascinating and valuable to me. I now consider design an essential element in a good drawing.

DESIGN ELEMENTS: WHAT TO LOOK FOR

When observing a figure for design potential, look for basic elements of design—straight, curved, simple, complex—as they apply to lines, shapes, masses, the body (both visible and concealed), clothing and a figure's gesture. As you look for these elements, try to look at the figure in a simpler form. Filter out complexities and look just at primary shapes and directions.

Straight or Curved?
Drawing 1 has straight design elements. Drawing 2 uses curved elements. Notice the difference of feeling between the two. If the elements are straight, are they static or dynamic? If they're curved, are they circular or are they flatter in some areas?

1

2

Simple or Complex?
The fold in drawing 3 is simple, and the folds in drawing 4 are complex and busy.

3

4

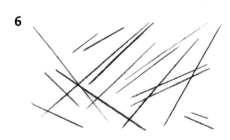

Static or Dynamic?
Static lines are vertical or horizontal (drawing 5). The closer lines are to static, the more calm and stable the effect. Dynamic lines are diagonal (drawing 6). The more severe a diagonal, the more active the impression.

5

6

Circular or Flat?
Some curves are arcs (drawing 7) and some are a bit flatter (drawing 8). Curves that have both circular and flat parts are often more beautiful and usually describe form more effectively than completely rounded curves.

7

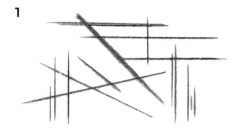

8

Contrast Creates Good Design
During a break, a model relaxed in this wonderful position. The straight parts of her figure contrast with her curve. Notice that every part of her figure has some elements that are more circular and some that are flatter. The static and horizontal line of her leg contrasts with many dynamic diagonal lines. The complexity of her face contrasts with the simplicity of the rest of her figure.

RELATE DESIGN TO CONTENT

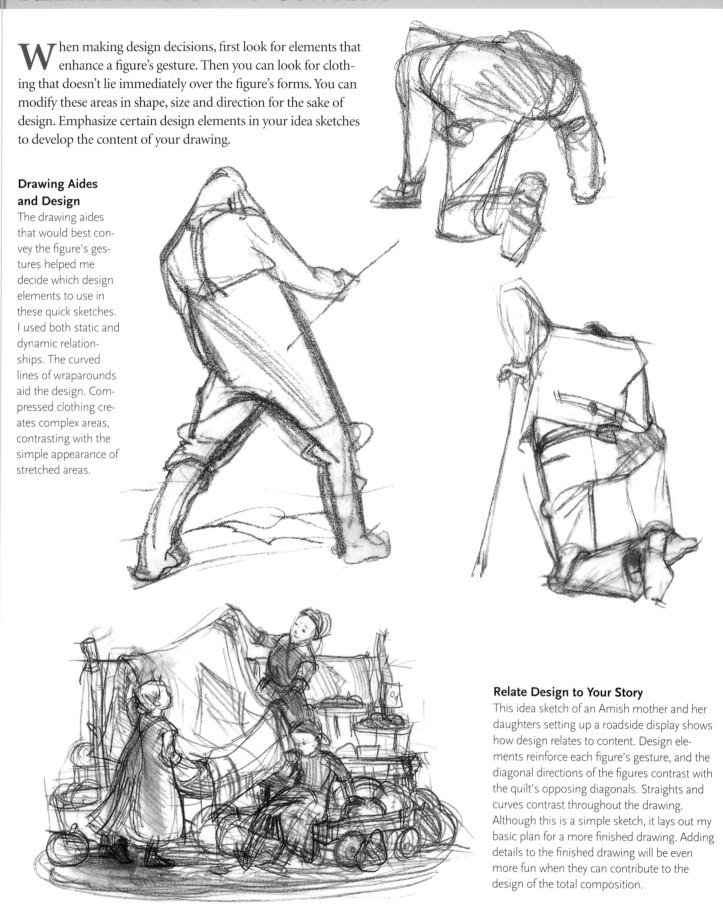

When making design decisions, first look for elements that enhance a figure's gesture. Then you can look for clothing that doesn't lie immediately over the figure's forms. You can modify these areas in shape, size and direction for the sake of design. Emphasize certain design elements in your idea sketches to develop the content of your drawing.

Drawing Aides and Design

The drawing aides that would best convey the figure's gestures helped me decide which design elements to use in these quick sketches. I used both static and dynamic relationships. The curved lines of wraparounds aid the design. Compressed clothing creates complex areas, contrasting with the simple appearance of stretched areas.

Relate Design to Your Story

This idea sketch of an Amish mother and her daughters setting up a roadside display shows how design relates to content. Design elements reinforce each figure's gesture, and the diagonal directions of the figures contrast with the quilt's opposing diagonals. Straights and curves contrast throughout the drawing. Although this is a simple sketch, it lays out my basic plan for a more finished drawing. Adding details to the finished drawing will be even more fun when they can contribute to the design of the total composition.

Consider Gesture and Design

Before beginning any sketch or drawing, look for the design elements that can both enhance the gesture of your subject or idea and also make an exciting design. Emphasize these in your drawing.

Primary Straights
Important horizontals and diagonals relate directly to the action of the body.

Secondary Straights
The diagonals under his left arm and under both legs reinforce his stretches. Though secondary, they are also exciting.

Curves Contrast Straights
The curves of clothing that wrap around his body reinforce his form and the directions of parts of his body while contrasting with the straight elements of his figure.

Simple Forms Contrast Complex Ones
Each pants leg has a simple side that contrasts with a side made complex by folds.

Avoid Parallels
Clothing free of the body offers opportunities for artistic license. I varied some diagonal lines from the model's actual gesture so they would not be parallel to others.

18

Drawing Heads and Hands

Viewers' eyes gravitate toward faces. The face, followed by the hands, is the most expressive part of a person. Though not every face may be considered beautiful according to the ideal of its culture, geographical place and time period, every face is unique and each has its own beauty. As artists, we appreciate the special quality of every face we encounter. As visual storytellers, we must have the ability to communicate the person we intend to show.

One can easily draw a face that looks different than intended. Learning how to place features on a head and realizing how perspective affects what you see will help you avoid misplacing features that can distort the face. Knowing what creates basic facial expressions, you can avoid depicting unintended ones. When you learn the symbols of aging, you'll be less likely to draw these effects on figures accidentally, making them appear older than you intended.

Interesting Bone Structure
This woman's face and bearing impressed me so much that I felt compelled to draw her. The bone structure underlying her features reflects her rare 100 percent Hawaiian ancestry.

THE STRUCTURE OF THE HEAD

To draw the head well, memorize the generic head proportions and the planes of the underlying skull. Skulls all have similar structures. It is by proportions that they differ.

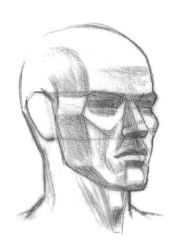

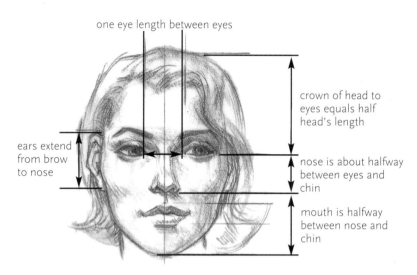

one eye length between eyes

crown of head to eyes equals half head's length

ears extend from brow to nose

nose is about halfway between eyes and chin

mouth is halfway between nose and chin

Structural Planes
Examine the planes of this generic head in a three-quarter view when lit from above. These planes reflect the planes of the skull.

Generic Proportions
Learn these proportions. Then you'll have a standard to which you can compare facial proportions of any individual you're drawing.

Use the Profile as a Template
Before drawing a person's head from any view, observe the proportions and characteristics of that individual from the side. Think of the profile as a template running down the face's center. From other views, you'll see this template in perspective.

Indicating Structure
To show the underlying structure of a head and to bring out the definition of its features, study the edges of the face and of its features. Study the edges of his eyes, nose and mouth and look for places where hard edges gradate to soft changes of plane.

THE STRUCTURE OF EYES

To successfully draw eyes, the most expressive of all features, study the generic structure. The eyeball fits into the socket, and the eyelids wrap over the eyeballs. The shape and proportions of the eye sockets and eyelids are the factors that vary between people.

1   **2**

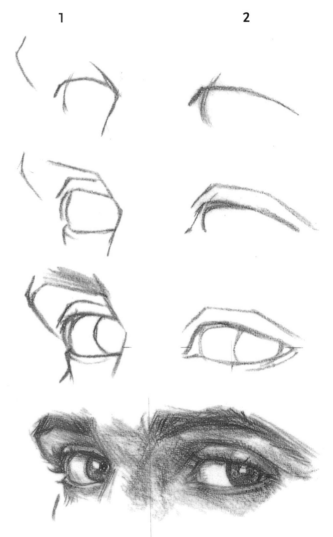

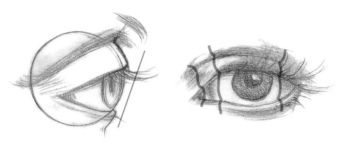

Generic Eye Structure

From the side, observe the thickness of the upper and lower eyelids and the diagonal relationship between the lids. From the front, be equally conscious of the form and thickness of the eyeball and eyelids.

Eyelid Curves

Note the high and low points of curves of the eyelid when viewed from different viewpoints, and look for the contrast between curved and straight areas.

Two Tricky Spots

When drawing three-quarter views of the eyes, pay attention to the far corner of each eye. To draw eye 1, first draw the edge of the nose, the edge of the eyeball and the overlapping upper lid. Next, add another line to indicate the thickness of each lid and then indicate the area where the lower lid wraps around the eyeball. To draw eye 2, first draw the eyeball edge. Draw another line to indicate the thickness of the upper lid. Last, draw the tear duct and then the lower lid.

THE STRUCTURE OF NOSES AND MOUTHS

Here are some tips for drawing noses and mouths.

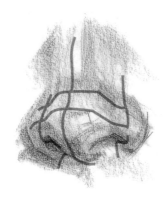

Observe the Planes on Mouths

No matter what shapes a person's nose and mouth are or what your perspective, study the features until you can draw lines to indicate different planes about every half inch, across and down their forms. Differentiate sharp changes of plane from curving transitions. The transition from skin to lip is a sharp change of plane close to the center of the mouth. The transition tapers to a soft curve closer to the edge of the mouth.

1

2

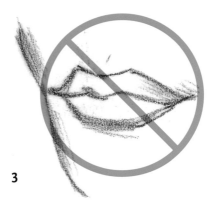

3

Notice Perspective, Even on Lips

When drawing a mouth at a three-quarter view, show the mouth's far corner as it wraps around the teeth. When viewing the mouth from below (drawing 1), the edge of the lower lip overlaps the upper lip at the corner. From above (drawing 2), the edge of the upper lip overlaps the lower lip at the far corner. Don't pull the corner out as in drawing 3. This prevents the lips from wrapping around the face, thus creating distortion.

Imagine Cross-Contour Lines

Each of these noses shows both sharp planes and soft curves. To understand the differing structures, visualize contour lines that run across and along each nose.

FACIAL EXPRESSIONS

All you need to draw facial expressions is a willingness to act them out. Make an expression you want to draw and study yourself in a mirror. Use a second mirror to study your profile, too. As you assume an expression, the muscles you use will tell you where your face has changed and where to look to observe these changes.

Notice the effect of eyes, eyelids and eyebrows on the face's expression. When the average viewer looks at a figure, he or she generally focuses on the face first. When the average viewer looks at the face, that person focuses on the eyes.

Eye Symbols
The more white that shows below the iris, the duller the face's expression. The more white that shows above the iris, the more excited the expression. Drawing 1 looks sleepy and bored. As the iris moves down, drawing 2 looks normal and alert. Drawing 3 is intense and staring at the viewer. Drawing 4 looks surprised, and drawing 5 looks frightened.

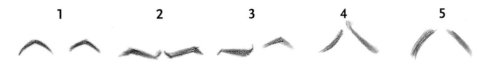

Eyebrow Symbols
Eyebrows convey almost as much expression as eyes do. Drawing 1 shows surprised eyebrows. They change to angry (drawing 2), puzzled (drawing 3), worried (drawing 4) and sad (drawing 5). Try to picture the eye expressions that would go with each set of eyebrows and try to make those expressions on your own face. Here's a hint for drawing procedure: If you're drawing angry, furrowed brows, begin with the brows and then draw the eyes. If you're drawing an expression with raised brows, draw the eyes first.

Eyes and Brows Working Together
In addition to paying attention to the placement of the iris within the eye and drawing expressive eyebrows, eyelid actions also can intensify expressions. When you add tone above the eyelid, use the eyebrow shapes as clues for the direction in which you should apply tone. Frightened eyes and surprised brows (drawing 1) indicate terror. Dull eyes and sad brows (drawing 2) look sick. Furrowed brows and narrow eyes (drawing 3) appear angry, even cruel. Angry brows with eyes that look to the side (drawing 4) seem suspicious. Eyes that look to the side with one raised eyebrow (drawing 5) are flirtatious, and one raised brow and one angry brow (drawing 6)—they just don't know what to think!

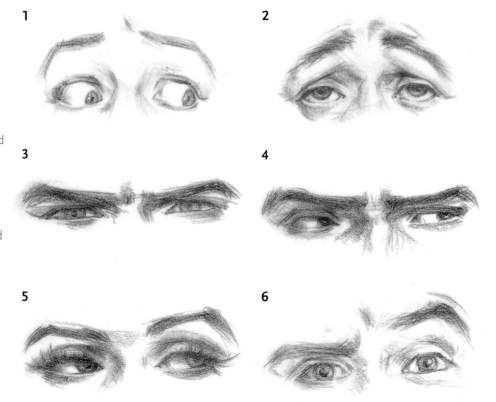

Mouths Wrap Around Teeth

In both open smiles and grins, mouths stretch around teeth until, at their corners, they are pulled away from the teeth and up by smiling cheeks. Eyes also look like they're smiling when the cheeks push up the lower eyelids. Show triangular dark areas inside the corners where the mouths are pulled away from the teeth, as on the far side of this mouth. Show accurate tooth edges and gum lines but underemphasize the detail and the value on the teeth.

1

2

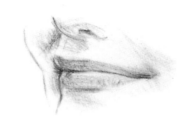

Drawing Grins

Draw the cheeks pulling up. Perspective affects the line at which the lips meet. Sometimes it curves up, as at eye level (drawing 1). When seen from below, though, it curves downward (drawing 2). However, no matter what your viewpoint, always make the corners turn up. Also soften the upper lip at each corner.

1

2

3

Combining Expressions

Surprised eyes and brows combine with a smilelike shout to indicate happy surprise (drawing 1). Raised brows, stretched upper eyelids, lowered eyes, pulled-up nostrils and a compressed mouth imply haughtiness and disdain (drawing 2). An expression with lifted brows, happy eyes looking to the side, a big grin and the head thrusted back show happy, triumphant pride (drawing 3).

HEADS IN PERSPECTIVE

When drawing heads from unusual views, make the relationships of features consistent with one another. Then use overlapping forms and wraparounds to reinforce these views. When drawing a head in perspective, determine the direction of a line drawn from one eyebrow to the others, usually a diagonal. Then be sure that any other line drawn across two symmetrical parts of the face is parallel to it.

1

2

Notice Changing Relationships and Shapes

The man in drawing 1 tilts his head downward and also to one side. This sideways tilt makes the relationships diagonal. In drawing 2, he tilts his head to the side, toward the viewer, and slightly back. Looking down on all his features as his head tilts also makes relationships between his features diagonal. Notice how the shape of each feature of the face changes when viewed from the different perspectives shown on this page.

3

4

5

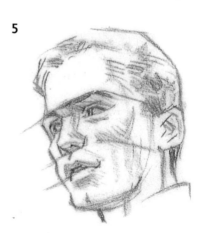

Observe Relationships Between the Nose, Eyes and Cheeks

Whenever you see a head from below, whether it's tilted back or your view is from a low point, pay special attention to two crucial relationships: between the bridge of the nose and the eyes and between the tip of the nose and the far cheek. The nose on drawing 3 is so concave that the bridge falls at the middle of the eyes. The bridge on drawing 4 is level with the top of her eye. The bridge on drawing 5 falls slightly above his eye. These relationships change when viewed from different perspectives. The placement of the tip of the nose and the cheekbone also are affected by the severity of your view, as well as the proportions of each face. Understanding your viewpoint can help you place the cheek and nose, and conversely, observing the relationship between the two can help you recognize the face's proportions and forms. The relationship between the nose and cheek is particularly apparent in ¾-views like these.

HAIR

Hair contributes to the personality of your characters and to the designs of your pictures. It adds texture and accents of value. I consider hair one of the most enjoyable parts of the figure to draw.

 **1**

 **2**

Hairline Shape
Think of the hairline shape as though it were drawn with hard edges (drawing 1). Note the space free of hair in front of and behind the ear. Use soft edges to draw the areas from which hair actually grows (drawing 2).

Use Hard Edges to Draw Overlaps
Think of hair in masses rather than strands. Draw overlapping masses with hard edges to define their shapes.

Light Hits a Mass of Hair as a General Form
Think of the entire mass of hair as a partial sphere as it receives light from a light source. Parts of the hair closest to the light source are lighter and those farther away or turning away from the light source will be in shadow. Curly hair also has small forms within the general shape that also receive light in their own ways. Curly hair also shows less contrast than straight hair. Think of straight hair as a plastic cap and curly hair as a wool cap. The general form of each cap receives light, but the fibers within a wool hat also receive light individually.

Concave and Convex Waves
Waves move not only from side to side, but also toward and away from the viewer. Add value to the curves that receive less light. Remember to follow the curve of the hairs with these strokes of value.

Create Depth With Masses
Look for groups of hairs, and then place one group behind another. To make them look more natural, draw the strands of hair within a group almost but not quite parallel.

DESIGN OF THE HEAD AND FACIAL FEATURES

S tudy the design of a head and its facial features to improve your ability to draw a resemblance.

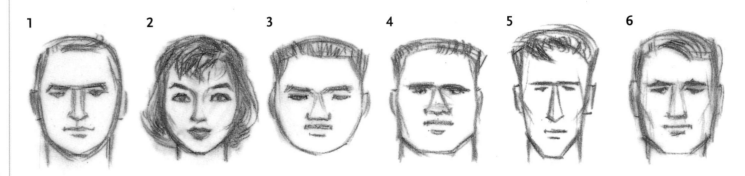

1   2   3   4   5   6

Front Face Shapes

The standard face shape (drawing 1) is an oval or egg shape. Compare the rest of these head shapes to the standard to better understand their unique designs. Drawing 2 is shaped like a heart, drawing 3 a circle, drawing 4 a square, drawing 5 a triangle and drawing 6 a rectangle.

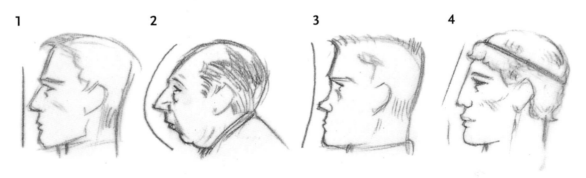

1   2   3   4

Profile Face Shapes

Also study the shape of each face's profile. Drawing 1 is unusually straight. Drawing 2 is birdlike, drawing 3 inside-out and drawing 4 Grecian.

Eye Relationships

When drawing a side view, pay special attention to the relationship between the front of the brow and the inner corner of the eye. As you can see, the degree of the slant can vary tremendously. Similarly, if you were viewing a face from the front, you should observe the relationship between the inner and outer corners of the eyes.

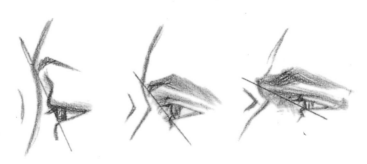

1

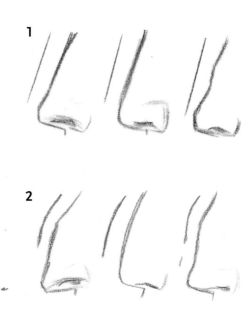

2

3

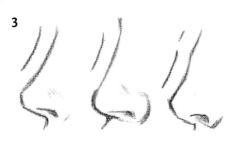

Profile Nose Shapes

The noses in row 1 are straight. Aquiline noses (row 2) are convex. Retroussé (French for turned up) noses (row 3) are concave. Many noses have bumps and depressions. Before drawing noses like this, determine the basic shape. Then add the details.

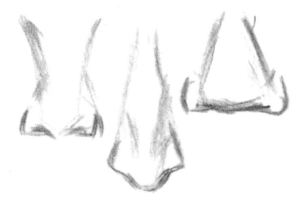

Front Nose Shapes

Squint your eyes so you can concentrate on the general shape of the nose. Does it resemble a triangle? If so, what are the proportions of the triangle? How wide is the base compared to the sides? Does the nose appear almost horizontal from nostril to nostril, or is there an angle between them?

Mouth Shapes

Observe the entire basic shape of the mouth. Compare the width to the height. Study the center lip line and how it relates to the corners. Look for the high points of the lips and for concave and convex curves.

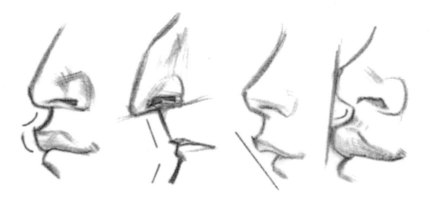

Relating the Mouth to the Nose

Observe the relationship between the upper and lower lips. Also pay attention to the shape between the upper lip and nose. Is it concave, convex or straight?

HANDS

Hands, through their ability to show action and emotion, play as important a part in storytelling as do faces. Hands are as varied as people are, and in their own way they all have character. Study the common characteristics of all hands to appreciate the differences between different people's hands.

1 **2**

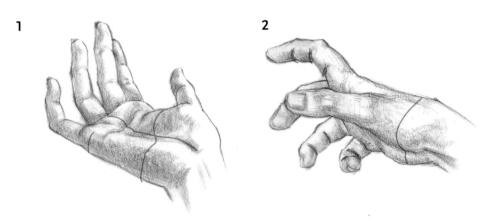

Study the Forms of Each Side
Draw contour lines across and around each finger and around and down the palm (drawing 1). Notice that the hand is thicker near the wrist than near the fingers. The palm of a relaxed hand is like a shallow cup. In drawing 2, notice that the thumb side of a hand is thicker than the little finger side. Observe how the creases under each finger wrap partially around the joint, showing its form and direction.

Study Your Own Hand
Each finger tapers at the top, and the group of fingers tapers toward the middle finger. The distance from your knuckle to the first joint is the same as the distance from the first joint to the tip of your finger. The first and third fingers are about the same length. The little finger comes up to the last joint of the third. The thumb's tip almost comes up to the first joint of the first finger. Your whole hand is approximately the same length as your face.

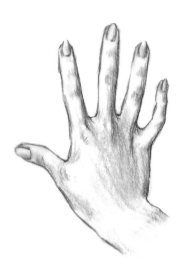

1 **2**

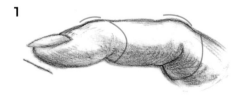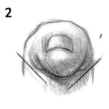

Form of Fingers
Notice the flatness of the side and underside of the finger compared to the rounded upper sides (drawing 1). There's a slight depression before and after each joint and a swell of flesh between the joints along the bottom of the finger. The tip of the finger as viewed from the side is diagonal, but viewed straight on (drawing 2), it's almost triangular. Notice how flat the lower part of the thumb is as it slopes diagonally toward the tip.

1   **2**

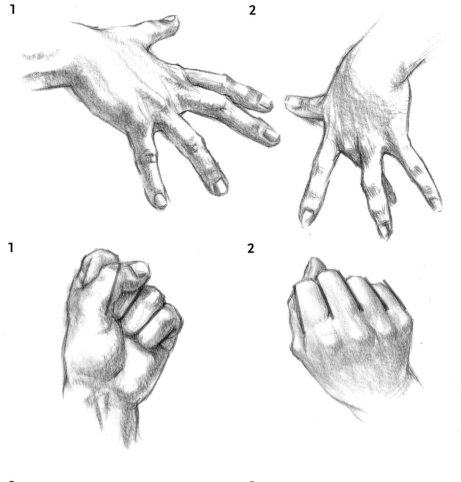

Men's and Women's Hands

To draw men's hands (drawing 1), make the knuckles more pronounced, make the tips of the fingers and nails angular, and emphasize the bone structure and tendons. To draw women's hands (drawing 2), taper the fingers, draw longer nails, model the hands delicately and downplay the knuckles and tendons.

1   **2**

Drawing Fists

Make a fist with your hand and observe how the folded fingers converge; the lines between the fingers are not quite parallel. From the palm side (drawing 1), they converge toward the center of the palm. From the back of the hand (drawing 2), they converge toward the upper knuckles. To emphasize the change of plane at the lower knuckles, vary the value and slightly darken each knuckle on one side.

1   **2**

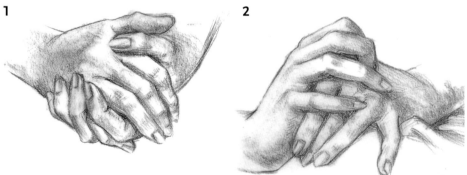

Hands Show Emotion

Even in the simple gesture of folding hands together, hands can show emotion. The hands in drawing 1 are in repose and express serenity. The folded hands in drawing 2 with two tense fingers imply nervousness.

EFFECTS OF AGING ON HEADS AND HANDS

As people age, their skin, particularly on faces, necks and hands, loses elasticity and stretches while the collagen and fat pads beneath the skin shrink. These factors, combined with a natural loss of moisture and the downward pull of gravity, cause wrinkles and droops of skin. Familiarity with these symbols of aging gives you the control to draw your people at the age you intend, rather than inadvertently drawing them older or younger than you want them to appear.

As artists, we have an advantage over many others. Instead of groaning at the inevitable signs of aging we see in the mirror, we also can study what we see for artistic purposes and say, "Well. Isn't that interesting?"

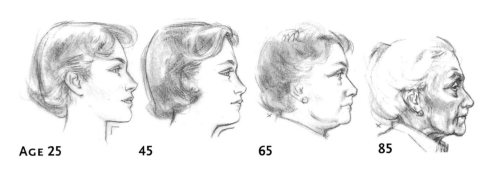

AGE 25   45   65   85

Learn These Changes of Profile

The most telling symbols of age in a profile are the neck and the changing relationship of the back of the neck to the face, caused by changing posture. These changes occur gradually. From ages twenty-five to forty-five, the front of the neck, the posture and the hair change. Ages sixty-five and eighty-five exhibit more differences.

A sharp change of angle from the chin to the throat is youthful. A long curve or sagging skin adds years. To draw younger people, clearly differentiate between the area under the chin and the throat. As men and women age, their carriage typically changes; the backs of their necks rise as their heads thrust forward. Men's necks thicken in middle age, which is particularly noticeable in the backs of their necks. In old age, their necks shrink, leaving sagging skin.

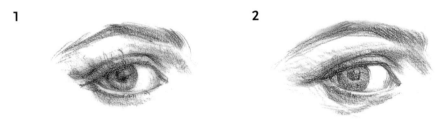

1   2

Critical Eye Areas

Drawing 1 is a younger eye. As skin stretches on the forehead, the skin below the eyebrows droops over the lid. Bags of lax skin and slipping fat appear under older eyes (drawing 2). Avoid excess modeling in these areas to prevent adding unwanted years to the face you're drawing.

1   2   3

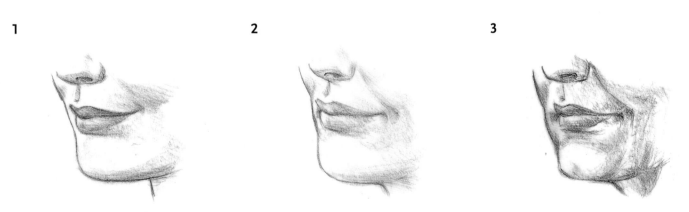

Critical Mouth and Chin Areas

The face in drawing 1 still has firm skin around the nose, mouth and neck. The corners of the mouth in drawing 2 are beginning to droop and the throat has started to curve. Drawing 3 shows a more developed fold of skin that begins at the nose and falls from the corner of the mouth almost to her chin. Don't model these areas too much unless you're drawing an older person.

AGE 25　　　　　　　　**65**　　　　　　　　**85**

Progression of Age

At twenty-five, the bone structure is visible but there are no wrinkles or sagging skin. By age sixty-five, the eyebrows and the skin below droop. Growing cartilage causes the nose and ears to grow. Middle-age weight gain causes the face to look fuller, and a fold of skin stretching from the nose and corner of the mouth to the chin appears. The mouth thins and drops at the corners. The neck thickens and folds of skin appear on the throat. By age eighty-five the head looks more skeletal. The eyeballs sink deeper into their sockets, causing deeper shadows around the eyes and the bridge of the nose. The nose and ears continue to grow. The cheekbones become more prominent as fat shrinks. The upper lip recedes, and the lips become thin and show wrinkles. More loose folds of skin appear on the thinning neck.

Back of the Neck

The backs of the necks of elderly people clearly show the effects of shrinking fat and loosening skin. Older people typically have a curved spine, which creates a head thrust and high back of the neck.

Drawing Aged Hands

Wrinkles of stretched skin are as evident on aged hands as on faces and necks. As collagen and fat pads shrink, knuckles, tendons and veins become more pronounced. Arthritis makes knuckles even larger and can distort fingers.

CHAPTER 19

Drawing Children

Drawing Children When They Pose
Older children often want to pose when they see you drawing others. It sometimes takes a little while for them to fall into their natural attitudes. You may want to wait to draw a posing child's shoulders and body until he or she has "settled in." Angles at the brow and cheekbones of this eight-year-old girl have started to show through. They indicate the beginnings of a beautiful bone structure.

Though it was not my intention to specialize in illustrating children, they have been the subjects of a large part of my professional work, and drawing them has brought me innumerable hours of pleasure. Almost everything you have learned about drawing people also applies to drawing children.

This chapter will focus on a few aspects of drawing children that differ from drawing other people. You'll learn how children differ from adults in body and head proportions. You'll learn how baby fat affects children's bodies, faces, and hands.

If you find drawing children difficult, don't become discouraged. Consider a sketching or drawing session successful even if you learned just a little more about drawing children. Be happy if you catch a few gestures you really like. Stick to sketching them and you'll find that you will learn more each time. That's when drawing children becomes a real treat.

COMPARING PROPORTIONS OF BABIES AND ADULTS

As children grow from infancy to adulthood, their muscles develop and their proportions change dramatically. You don't have to memorize children's proportions from one year to the next, but it is important to be sensitive to proportional changes from one stage to the next.

You already know the ideal body and head proportions of an adult. Now, as a point of reference, learn the body and head proportions of a one year old, the age by which most children can stand. You then can observe and appreciate the fascinating physical developments between one year and twenty-one years.

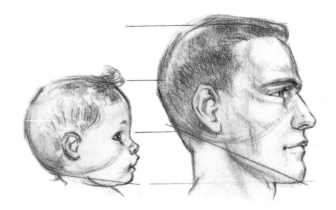

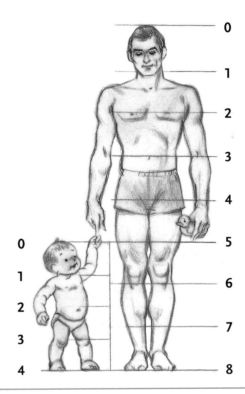

Compare Head Proportions

The baby's head is already about two-thirds the size of an adult's head even though his body is only three-eighths his father's height. Compare the relationship of each person's cranium to his chin. The diagonal from the lower back cranium to the chin of the twenty-one year old is much more extreme, showing how much his face has lengthened.

Compare Body Proportions

Divide each figure's body into sections equal to the height of his head. The twenty-one year old's height is equal to eight lengths of his head. The one year old's height equals four lengths of his head.

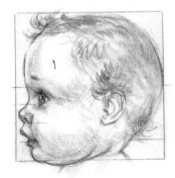
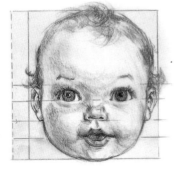

Baby Head Proportions

This baby's profile is close to a square. The full face is similar but slightly rounder. If you divide the head into two horizontal parts, you'll notice that the forehead up to the crown of the head forms one half while the eyes down form the other half. If you divide the lower half into four more parts, you'll notice that the lines define the bottoms of the eyes, nose, lips and chin.

When drawing adults, you learned that the space between the eyes is equal to the width of one eye. On a baby, the space between the eyes is larger. The bridge of the nose is shallow, so avoid applying too much tone from the eye to the bridge. Note how fat the cheeks are and that they reach down to the chin and sometimes farther.

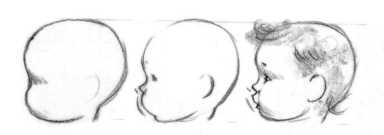

Steps to Drawing a Baby Profile

Think curves and think rounded areas. Notice the thrusting mouth area and the diagonals of the mouth and the nose; the baby's face is designed for suckling.

Draw two curves, the top one a little longer than the bottom one. Remember to think of the baby's head in terms of a general square. Draw the rest of the cranium to fill the square. Then draw a short, upturned nose, a rounded mouth area and a tiny chin. Last, add upper and lower lips to the rounded mouth area, indicate the eyes and ears and add a little hair.

Baby Fat

For almost the first twelve months of their lives, healthy babies acquire fat—on their faces, bodies, legs, arms, hands, feet, everywhere—that they gradually lose with age as they grow taller and their muscles and physical skills develop. By about age seven, little fat remains and you may notice it only in their cheeks, hands and bellies. When drawing generic young children, look for fat and show it!

On Faces
This baby has fat everywhere. His cheeks are so fat that a big smile merely creates little folds near his mouth. This is characteristic of smiles on young children.

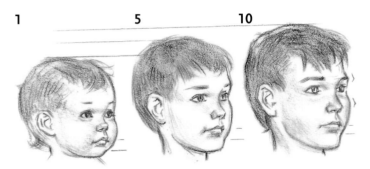

Fat Decreases With Age
In a baby you see only curves. By ten, as fat is diminishing, angles may appear at the brow and cheek. Note the spot where the curve of the cheek ends and the curve of the chin begins. The farther below the mouth this spot occurs, the younger the child appears.

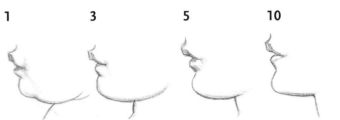

Draw Convex Chins
Always draw the curve under a child's chin convex, never concave. Babies and small children even have overlapping folds between the chin and neck. A ten year old may have lost fat, but the angle between the chin and throat is still defined.

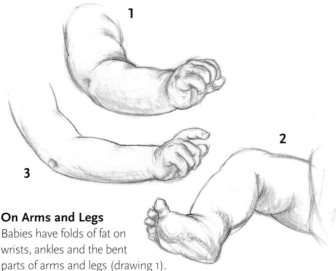

On Arms and Legs
Babies have folds of fat on wrists, ankles and the bent parts of arms and legs (drawing 1). You see dimples instead of bones at the elbow. There are extra folds between the shoulder and the elbow and between the elbow and the wrist. Similar folds appear on babies' legs (drawing 2). Folds generally disappear as children grow older, but fat continues to affect the arm for several years (drawing 3).

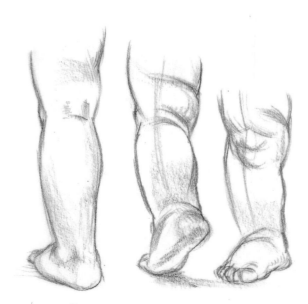

Fat On Standing Legs
Baby legs have folds between the knees and groin. These folds decrease as the child grows, but you'll see hints of them for several years.

FLEXIBILITY

The bodies of children are wonderfully flexible, so before sketching a child's gesture, determine what the spine is doing. It probably will be arched, with the chest and stomach thrusting forward, or curved with the chest compressed against the stomach.

1

2

3

Rounded Bellies

Healthy babies have protruding, round little bellies that may not completely disappear until puberty. Drawing 1 shows a child with its chest thrust forward, an easy stretch to draw. Drawing 2 shows a baby with a rounded back and its chest compressed against its round belly. Don't draw a baby with both the back and chest bulging (drawing 3).

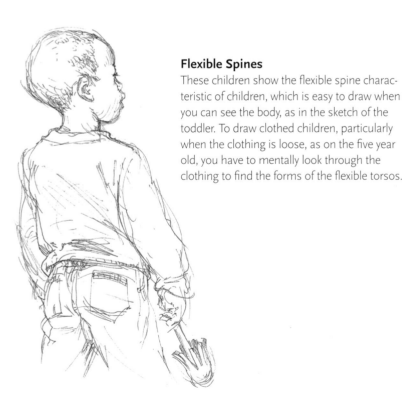

Flexible Spines

These children show the flexible spine characteristic of children, which is easy to draw when you can see the body, as in the sketch of the toddler. To draw clothed children, particularly when the clothing is loose, as on the five year old, you have to mentally look through the clothing to find the forms of the flexible torsos.

HINTS FOR DRAWING CHILDREN

The slender, short necks characteristic of children seem to emphasize their vulnerability. To make sure the neck looks slender and to bring out the round shape of the cranium, always relate the front of the neck to the chin and draw the front first. Then, relate the back of the neck to the front.

1

2

Longer Necks Indicate Older Age

To show how important a neck can be, I drew exactly the same face on these little girls. The longer neck of the girl in drawing 2, along with a new hair style, make her look a good year older than the girl in drawing 1. Notice that her cheek extends almost to her chin.

1

2

3

Teeth

When drawing open smiles on children, pay attention to the same areas as when drawing adult smiles: the shapes of the teeth and gums and the dark triangles inside the corners of the mouth. Notice the difference in size and shape of the baby teeth of the five year old (drawing 1) and the adult teeth of the eight year old (drawing 3). A missing front tooth is so typical of a seven year old (drawing 2) that you can use it to indicate that age.

Hands and Feet

Think curves! Some of the fat in babies' hands and feet remains well into children's school years. Observe in these drawings how padded the bone areas are. Unless sharply bent, knuckles still appear as dimples. Note the curving overlaps of flesh and the places where convex curves meet to form angles between them. Tone can reinforce the fatness of fingers.

USING DRAWING AIDES TO DRAW CHILDREN

It's a given: Unless they're sleeping, I expect young children to move so quickly from one attitude to the next that you have little time to draw their actions. In one glance, try to take in as much you can—torso action, head action, attitude and rhythms of legs and arms all the way through the hands or feet. The more you know about drawing adults, the more quickly you can draw children.

Prioritize

I wanted to capture this baby's face before he moved, so I concentrated on that area. I also had time to partially sketch his gestures. Note the continuity of his arms all the way through the stretched sides of his wrists in both sketches. In quick sketches, even without drawing fingers, the bend of a wrist or the weight resting on a hand can help tell the story of the figure. This baby seemed to like his shirt just as it was, pulled partly off.

Using Drawing Aides

Rhythm, stretch and compression, and overlapping forms—great for indicating baby fat—were particularly valuable in catching the gestures of these toddlers. You may not be able to finish sketching many gestures you start; that's OK as long as you're observing and learning.

HINTS FOR SKETCHING CHILDREN ON LOCATION

Children move and fidget a lot, but there are opportunities to catch a gesture. Children often repeat gestures or switch back and forth between them. You also can sketch them while in thought or even sleeping. If a child is moving, try to remember the gesture and look for drawing aides, especially rhythm and wraparounds, that will help you draw that gesture.

Catch Children in Thought
This girl was concentrating so hard that she didn't even realize I was drawing her. This gave me enough time to draw her sweet face and the way she hugged her old bear.

Look For Repetitive Actions
Even though children fidget a lot, they often repeat gestures often enough to give you more than one glance or chance to catch it. After a child has moved, you can add the little details that bring the picture together. This little boy went back and forth between eating his lunch and rocking his chair.

Look for Drawing Aides
As this gangly boy got out of a swimming pool, he wrapped his arms around himself and shivered. Being aware of the rhythms through his figure helped me catch his fleeting gesture.

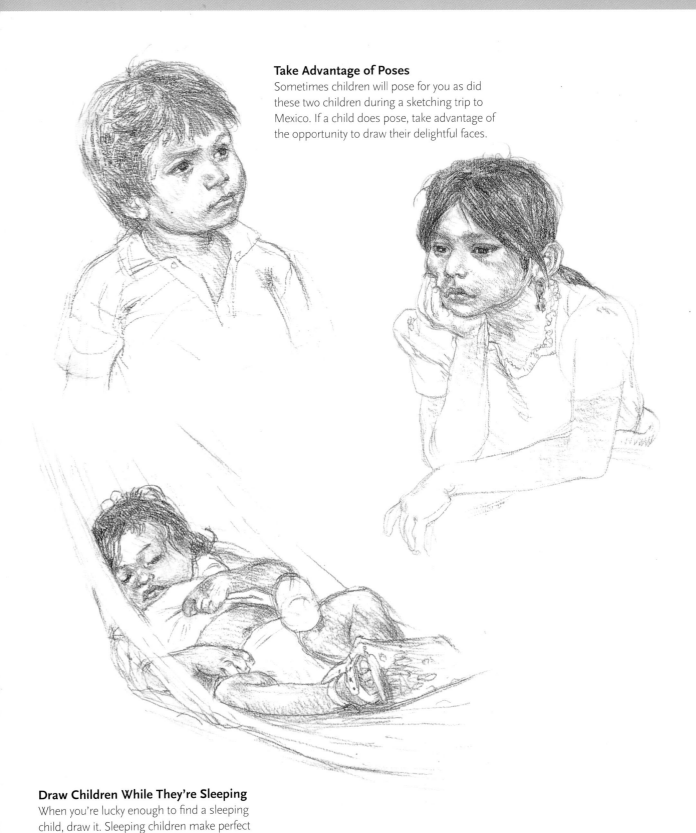

Take Advantage of Poses
Sometimes children will pose for you as did these two children during a sketching trip to Mexico. If a child does pose, take advantage of the opportunity to draw their delightful faces.

Draw Children While They're Sleeping
When you're lucky enough to find a sleeping child, draw it. Sleeping children make perfect models: They don't fidget or really move at all.

GLOSSARY

Apparent Relationship a relationship of or between parts of a figure as seen from your viewpoint

Aquiline describing a convex curve, usually used in reference to noses

Attitude a figure's posture in relation to action or mood

Bias describing fabric cut diagonally to its weave, as opposed to straight

Cast Shadow the shadow cast by a form onto other surfaces

Clean describing sharp or crisp edges within a drawing

Compression the state of a part of a body being compressed or squeezed, as opposed to stretched, in a gesture

Compressed Folds the folds that appear in compressed areas of fabric, often over compressed areas of the figure beneath

Concave describing the inner face of a curve

Continuity a state of uninterrupted form, whether a line, figure or part of a figure

Contrapposto an opposition of contrasting masses, usually applying to a twisting torso

Convex describing the outer face of a curve

Core Shadow the darkest part of the shadow on a form; the part that receives the least light

Design the harmonious arrangement of elements in a drawing

Diaper Fold a fold that appears in the area of fabric that slacks or sags between two points of support

Direct Drawing a drawing done without an underdrawing of lines or tone

Drawing Aide an analytical device that helps artists observe and draw figures to bring out attitude, action and form

Drop Fold a fold that falls free from one point of support

Dynamic giving the effect of movement, associated with diagonal forms

Factual Relationship a true relationship of or between parts of a figure as seen from the front at eye level, unaffected by perspective

Foreshortening a phenomenon of perspective by which a form appears shorter when viewed in perspective than it is in reality

Gathers the source of folds of fabric that is compressed or gathered together

Grounded convincingly appearing to stand on a surface

Half-Lock Fold a fold that occurs when a tubular area of fabric bends abruptly, such as the sleeve around a bending elbow

Highlight the lightest part of a form, the part that receives the most light

Illustrative Drawing a drawing that has a narrative quality

Inert Fold a mass of fabric with one or several folds that remains inactive

Overlapping Form a part of the body or fabric that overlaps another

Perspective the phenomenon that makes identical forms look different from varied points of view

Pipe Fold a conical or cylindrical-shaped fold that occurs when fabric falls free from a gathered source or stretches between two sources

Planes a term used to indicate flat areas of a form that face different directions

Proportion the relationship of sizes between two parts of a whole or between one part and the whole

Reflected Light light on an object's shadow area that has bounced back onto its form from another surface

Relationship imaginary line between parts of a figure or between a part of the figure and the ground; relationships can be factual or apparent

Retroussé describing a concave curve, usually in reference to noses

Rhythm the flow or curved line through the center or part of a figure

Spiral Fold a fold that forms when a tubular piece of fabric is compressed, such as the sleeve of a shirt that is pushed up

Squeeze Pose a figure's position in which the torso compresses on one side and stretches on the other

Static giving the effect of stillness, associated with vertical and horizontal forms

Straight describing fabric cut along the length or width of its weave, as opposed to bias

Stretch Fold a fold that forms over the stretching part of a figure

Tangent the appearance of two lines or edges touching one another, which causes these forms to lose their forms or look two-dimensional

Thumbnail a rough compositional sketch, usually drawn small, to establish a picture's basic elements

Wraparound an element of the body or of clothing that wraps around or follows the form of the figure beneath

Value the degree of a tone's darkness or lightness

Zigzag Folds folds that make a zigzag pattern, often occurring on the inside of the bend of a tubular piece of fabric

You Can Sketch Almost Anywhere
This is one of the many inflight sketches I drew thirty thousand feet in the air while sitting in the cockpit of a C-141 Starlifter thanks to the long-standing cooperative program between the U.S. Air Force and many national illustrator societies.

A PARTING NOTE

Those who are or wish to become professional artists or those who draw or paint for relaxation can anticipate hard work, much trial and error, some confusion and frequent frustration. However, the satisfaction of accomplishment and meeting challenges brings rewards far greater than any frustration. It also brings pleasure and occasional joy. Those who love to draw are fortunate in many ways. As long as there is someone or something to observe, we are never without resources. We can even draw in our heads. And there is so much to learn about drawing that we can continue learning our entire lives. It is my hope that you have learned much from these pages, that they have helped you enjoy the challenge of drawing people and that you will continue to learn throughout your life.

ABOUT THE AUTHOR

Following her education at the University of California at Berkeley and at the Art Center College of Design in Pasadena, Barbara Bradley (then known as Barbara Briggs) spent the first years of her professional life in illustration at Charles E. Cooper Studios in New York. After returning to the San Francisco Bay Area, she freelanced as an artist, winning many national awards in illustration. She also began teaching at the Academy of Art College, becoming director of illustration for more than twenty-five years until her semiretirement. For her work at the academy, she was named Outstanding Vocational Educator by the College Career Association in 1992. She has taught drawing workshops in London, at Pixar and at Disney Animation Studios in Burbank, California, and Orlando, Florida. Today, Mrs. Bradley is a consultant at the Academy of Art College, where she also teaches drawing of her favorite subjects: expressive people, characters and children. She does occasional illustration and sketches and paints for pleasure. Her work is in several private collections, corporate offices, the Museum of American Illustration at the Society of Illustrators and the permanent collection of the U.S. Air Force.

INDEX

THE BEST IN ART INSTRUCTION COMES FROM NORTH LIGHT BOOKS!

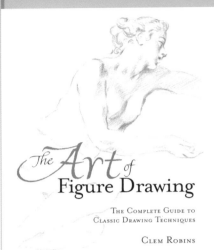

Clem Robins shows you how to render accurate human figures in the elegant style of the old masters. Distilling his lifetime of experience into a complete figure drawing course, Robins provides special step-by-step guidelines for drawing heads, hands, hair and feet. You'll also learn how to draw from life, transforming what you see into realistic, classically rendered images.

ISBN 1-58180-204-8, paperback, 144 pages, #31984-K

Discover the limitless creative possibilities of colored pencils! Janie Gildow shows you how to mix colored pencils with watercolor, pastel, acrylic, ink and more. Gorgeous galleries, inspirational art and twenty-four step-by-step demonstrations showcase a stunning variety of creative combinations.

ISBN 1-58180-186-6, hardcover, 144 pages, #31956-K

Here's all the instruction you need to create beautiful, luminous paintings by layering with watercolor. Linda Stevens Moyer provides straightforward techniques, step-by-step mini-demos and must-have advice on color theory and the basics of painting light and texture—the individual parts that make up the "language of light."

ISBN 1-58180-189-0, hardcover, 128 pages, #31961-K

Discover the elegance and beauty of Chinese brush painting! Renowned painter Kwan Jung shows you how to master this age-old style of painting. You'll learn how to create the unique brush-stroke techniques along with composition, perspective, mood and more. Twelve fun, easy-to-follow demonstrations provide guidelines for painting orchids, mums, bamboo, pandas, horses and more.

ISBN 1-58180-207-2, hardcover, 128 pages, #31985-K

Combine your passions for travel and painting by creating beautiful watercolor sketchbooks of the trips you take, capturing the places, people and events you never want to forget. Inside you'll find easy-to-use techniques for painting a sketchbook on the road—one you'll want to keep and show your family and friends.

ISBN 1-58180-272-2, hardcover, 128 pages, #32143-K

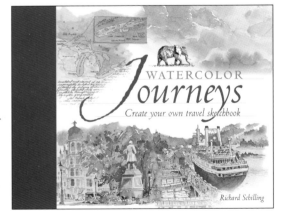

These books and other fine North Light titles are available from your local art & craft retailer, book store, online supplier or by calling 1-800-448-0915 in North America or 0870 2200220 in the UK.